The Responsible Campus

Studies in Christian Higher Education

Number 14

THE RESPONSIBLE CAMPUS:

Toward a New Identity

for the

Church-Related College

By CHARLES S. McCoy

1972
Division of Higher Education
Board of Education, The United Methodist Church
Nashville, Tennessee

294035

TO THE MEMORY OF MY MOTHER
(1887-1972)

CONTENTS

PREFACE

THE RESPONSIBLE CAMPUS: TOWARD A NEW IDENTITY FOR THE CHURCH-RELATED COLLEGE represents an attempt to view the problems and possibilities of church-related colleges in the perspective of theology and ethics. The book has evolved over several years in presentations at campus ministry conferences, in speeches to gatherings of educators, and in a series of papers for the Council on the Church-Related College. Having benefited greatly from comments and criticisms of participants in these meetings, I hope that the publication of these ideas will continue to evoke lively and fruitful discussion.

For permission to quote from various works, I express my thanks. All biblical quotations are from the Revised Standard Version.

Richard N. Bender bears heavy responsibility for this book, if not for the content, at least for encouraging me to prepare it and for its publication. Paul Mininger read an earlier draft and was helpful to me on many points. Mrs. Clyde Wilson-Reid and Mrs. Philip Woodworth have performed faithfully the secretarial tasks of the project. My daughter, Priscilla, aided in the task of correcting the galley proofs. Most of all, I express appreciation to my wife, Marjorie, whose constructive suggestions, tireless work, and loving encouragement enabled me to complete it.

CHARLES S. MCCOY

Tübingen, Germany
October 23, 1972

INTRODUCTION

NEVER BEFORE has there been as much soul-searching, as much in-depth inquiry, regarding the viability of church-related higher education as now. No issue before the church is of graver concern nor more fraught with "portents for the soul"—the soul of the church, and the soul of every educational enterprise, whether church-related or not. For this reason if for no other (and there are others), this is a timely book. It should be studied with care by every churchman and by every educator who takes his task seriously.

This is a thought-provoking and controversial book. In the present plethora of published materials, no other kind of book deserves attention from people whose time is valuable. These words are from Dr. McCoy's statement of his basic thesis:

> The church-related college today finds itself in a crisis of identity, caught between its sectarian past and its public present. It must act responsibly in terms of this public present if it is to fulfill its Christian heritage and survive as a meaningful part of American higher education.

By his analysis of what that responsibility is, the reader will find himself enlightened and challenged. This is not a book to be easily ignored when its far-reaching implications are grasped. Some will react to it with strong affirmation, others with grave reservations. Be that as it may, the reader will find himself confronted with ideas that demand he make up his mind. While it is my purpose here to introduce the book rather than to review it, some brief noting of several of the topics possessing "provocation potential" will help to anticipate adequately what is ahead.

1. Significantly, controversy over this book will emerge from both the right and the left. Many who are strongly committed to church-related higher education will be disturbed, particularly in the early chapters, by the searching critique to which the author submits

13

church-related colleges. Not only does he note serious weaknesses; he states them more cogently than do many detractors of such colleges. Those who already have written off church-related colleges will be at least equally disturbed to discover that, having taken account of the worst that can be said, Dr. McCoy builds a solid case for the importance of such colleges in the present and future.

2. In almost any extended discussion of church-related colleges, one of the early questions raised is, "After all, in just what way is the church-related college unique?" This is a crucial question, and an unavoidable one. One of the most controversial sections of the book develops around the author's stance that there is no such uniqueness, and that the very question itself is illegitimate. With considerable justification, it can be held that after proving the church-related college cannot be unique and showing that the question is asked for the wrong reasons, he proceeds throughout the remainder of the book to show that these colleges really are unique! Denying they are unique in essence, he asserts that they may exhibit a highly important "operational uniqueness."

3. Another question raised in recent years with growing persistence is whether there are valid theological foundations for church involvement in higher education. Asked differently, the question might be, "Is there anything in the essential nature of the Christian faith itself that entails church-related higher education?" After much searching, many protagonists have concluded that while there are important pragmatic reasons for such involvement, there are no theological grounds. By contrast, Dr. McCoy, drawing on his competence as both theologian and educator, builds a formidable case *for* theological foundations. At the heart of this theological interpretation is what the author calls "the incarnational perspective."

> It is this incarnational perspective that makes possible a view of a church-related college as called in Christian faith to abandon pretensions to uniqueness and to address the tasks set by human needs and aspirations. A new identity, one consistent with both Christian faith and social responsibility, can be discovered through affirming solidarity with creation, society, and the human condition.

The search for theological foundations is by no means an exercise in deduction from a priori presuppositions. Rather, the method is inductive, closely correlated with a competent analysis of the present

14

milieu of higher education and brilliant insight regarding the special functional opportunities open to contemporary church-related higher education. Herein there is special attention given to what the author calls "the fourth dimension" of higher education—that of ethical inquiry and critical evaluation.

4. No problem in the present higher educational scene has been of more pressing concern than that of adequate theory and practice of governance. Dr. McCoy proposes a "community of authority" as a basic principle, to be founded on the communal nature of the person and of the Christian faith. He sees the student as a genuine participant in the decision-making process, while not holding that policy and practice should be determined solely by a majority vote of the student body. Some will react to this as hopelessly idealistic; some may think it more practical than any alternatives now in view.

5. In recent years there has been, quite properly, much debate about whether an educational institution should be involved deliberately in social change. Dr. McCoy takes the position that as a matter of unavoidable fact the college *is* so involved, and if it were not it should be. The only fruitful questions would include what kind of change, how, and to what ends. These questions are the rub.

Perhaps the most valuable single characteristic of the book is that it is not simply another competent analysis of the present higher educational picture with a new statement of questions that have been asked and reasked long since. It moves far beyond this point to concrete proposals for constructive response and meaningful change. Dr. McCoy sees clearly that not only proposals and procedures are called for; he asserts the indispensability of commitment, expertise, and leadership. I doubt that either churchman or educator can read this work through without feeling a strange thrill, an almost fearful challenge to the special role the church and college working together can fulfill in the human needs of our time.

In brief, we have here a major contribution to current thought and discussion on the present and future of church-related colleges.

A few comments regarding the circumstances out of which this book emerges are pertinent. At one time, the Division of Higher Education of The United Methodist Church sponsored a task force known as the Council on the Church-Related College. The council was made up of a carefully chosen group of college presidents, faculty members, deans, and churchmen who are interested in higher education but who are not professional educators. Numbering twenty-two persons, the council met biennially over a five-year period. Its purpose was not to focus on "how to" but upon "whether" and "why." It undertook to identify the questions most centrally important to a raison d'etre of church-related colleges and to examine such questions thoroughly and dispassionately.

Typically, council members prepared position papers on the topics selected for each meeting. These were submitted to thoroughgoing criticism in sessions of sufficient length to permit searching examination. The intent was not to produce public-relations statements in simple capsulated form. Such statements have their appropriate place, but this was not the assignment of the council, which would be described by some as "hardheaded." The intent was not to destroy the ground for church-related higher education, but to find ground that is solid. Oversimplified analysis, superficial answers, or the employment of nonsequiturs makes no contribution to the need to which the council sought to respond. Neither was it the purpose of the council to produce a dogma to which the colleges were asked to conform. United Methodism is inescapably pluralistic and, if anything, the colleges related to it are even more so. No dogmatic philosophy of higher education could hope to be acceptable either in church or college. Identification of pertinent questions, searching discussion, and ventures toward insight emerging from a forum of competent and concerned churchmen and educators—these have been the goals.

Various of the working papers prepared originally for the council have been published in journals, periodicals, and symposia. They have been quoted widely in many other essays, some inspired by council papers. Early in 1971, the division published a selection of these papers under my editorship, entitled *The Church-Related College Today: Anachronism or Opportunity?*

The major literary production associated with the work of the council is *The Responsible Campus: Toward a New Identity for the Church-Related College.* No brief needs to be present supporting Dr. McCoy's qualifications to produce such a book. As Robert Gordon Sproul Professor of Religion in Higher Education at the Pacific School of Religion, he is doubtless the most respected scholar at work in this significant field. His former students fill many places of responsibility in higher education. While what is written here is finally Dr. McCoy's work, it is significant to note that the entire manuscript was discussed in great detail at several meetings of the Council on the Church-Related College (of which he is a member). Few books ever coming to print have had more benefit from the refining fire of searching criticism. Dr. McCoy's book incorporates the sharpened insights of a first-rate scholar responding to the critique of a competent community of concern. It is not surprising that what is said here regarding the spirit and method of the council is reflected in this book. Thus circumstances have conspired to produce an important work on a crucial topic at a critical time by the right author.

Perhaps a concluding personal word is pertinent also. Since 1953, I have been a member of the staff of the United Methodist Division of Higher Education. While my specific responsibilities have shifted from time to time and finally encompassed a rather broad spectrum, I have had an unbroken service relationship to educational institutions related to the church. I have learned to know all of them well, many of them quite intimately. I have participated with them in their search for a new identity. I have had the opportunity also to see them as part of the total higher educational enterprise, and to make sober evaluations regarding their value to the church and to the culture generally. My firm conviction is that the church, if it takes its mission to our time seriously, cannot afford to lose its relationship to a family of educational institutions. Wherever the church is at work, and at whatever expressions of its mission, it must be able to call on the services of a laity and clergy that are thoroughly competent and deeply committed to the cause of Christ in the world. To sever this relationship or to allow it to atrophy would be the greatest of folly. The colleges, if they are to be true to their own heritage and nature, must have the support of a community of faith that understands what the colleges are about and is committed to help them fulfill their purposes. I have been among the most privileged of men to have an opportunity to invest myself in a cause of this magnitude. Among the many projects in which I have been involved with the Division of Higher Education, I regard the work of the Council on the Church-Related College as one of the most significant, and this book as its major undertaking.

RICHARD N. BENDER

Nashville, Tennessee

17

Chapter I

THE DILEMMA OF THE CHURCH-RELATED COLLEGE

MY THESIS can be stated simply: the church-related college today finds itself in a crisis of identity, caught between its sectarian past and its public present. It must act responsibly in terms of this public present if it is to fulfill its Christian heritage and survive as a meaningful part of American higher education. In the first place, a solution of this nature means acceptance of its sectarian past as a source both of serious difficulties and of exciting possibilities. In the second place, it means facing the changing constituencies and sources of financing as challenges to rethink the purposes and potentialities in terms of which it must respond today. And third, it means exploring and exploiting the opportunities inherent in the present situation rather than attempting to continue outmoded patterns and expectations inherited from the nineteenth century or engaging in an orgy of hand wringing over the apparently disadvantageous position of the church-related college today.

While it seems clear that some church-related colleges are superfluous, it must also be emphasized that church-related institutions may play a vital and significant role in higher education, and that it would be a catastrophe of major proportions to American society and the Christian movement if the churches withdrew from this crucial sector of education. The point at issue is how each college may become a responsible campus in this time of rapid change and revolution of global proportions.

19

1. Death and Resurrection

A funny thing happened to the old Christian college on the way to the cemetery. Pronounced dead in authoritative quarters and prepared for burial, it unexpectedly began to show signs of life. New life in the supposed corpse has come as a shock to many, especially those who had predicted an early death. Admittedly, the resurrected body often bears little resemblance to the old being, but the vital functions are present, and continuity with the past can be detected.

Even more surprising than the new life, however, is that the potentialities of the church-related college may prove instructive for all American higher education, from small private colleges to large universities. Precisely because the church-related college has become marginal in the twentieth century, its problems and possibilities reflect in magnified form crucial dilemmas faced by higher learning as a whole.

All has not gone well with denominational colleges as they have been caught up in the explosive expansion of American higher education during the present century. As had been the fate of most denominational colleges in the nineteenth century, many of the surviving ones appear destined for the casualty list. The tremendous growth of public higher education has eclipsed in prestige and financial resources all but an "upper crust" of nonpublic institutions.

Churchmen, public administrators, and foundation officials have often taken the position that it remained only to prepare suitable obituary notices for these anachronistic institutions still struggling along under religious auspices. Some ecclesiastical boards responsible for denominational colleges have not only often recommended the severing of relation between church and college but also have at times been on the verge of recommending that their denominations withdraw completely from the support of all institutions of higher education.

Like old soldiers, however, the church-related colleges refused to die; but most of them were fading away. Then the process of renewal began. The G.I. Bill and the general rush for a college degree after the second world war gave new life to them. Federal funds for residence halls and classroom buildings provided further transfusions. The wake, we may say, ended when the corpse sat up in the coffin and demanded treatment.

2. The Changing Scene of Higher Education

Far-reaching transformations have occurred in American colleges and universities over the past century. Among the most obvious is sheer growth—in curricular offerings, in number of institutions, in size of faculties, in research, in student enrollment, in budgets, and in the hugeness of individual universities. Within the colleges, the courses available and disciplines of study have multiplied. Even more sweeping, however, has been the rapidly expanding scope of university research and instruction so that "the higher learning now addresses itself to the totality of . . . life, not just to its intellectual aspect." [1] This expansion has resulted in no small measure from the increase of funds from state and federal sources that has led higher education toward concern for every facet of man's life. The results include not only improvements in agriculture and industry but also the development of fantastic power and technological innovation amounting to a second industrial revolution. From being a passive transmitter of tradition, higher education has become a dynamic source of change and a major influence in shaping society. Colleges and universities are a prime national resource, whether one considers military, political, economic, or cultural power.

There is no reason to think that change in society or on campus will stop; instead, the speed of change will probably accelerate. Warren Bryan Martin suggests "that learning in the twenty-first century will take place under arrangements so radically different from present educational forms that the ways we do things now are not likely to have much transfer value then" and "that the content of educational programs in the future will be changed no less radically than the forms; indeed, changed to such an extent that what we teach today may be regarded by educators in the next century as negative precedents—examples of what not to do." [2] Students today have already been saying as much.

Church-related higher education has shared in the dramatic changes that have occurred over the past century. And the result is even less reassuring. The church-related college appears to many observers as an anachronism. For one thing, church colleges today attract a far

---

[1] John S. Brubacher and Willis Rudy, *Higher Education in Transition.* New York: Harpers, 1958, p. 374.

[2] Warren Bryan Martin, *Alternative to Irrelevance: A Strategy for Reform in Higher Education.* Nashville: Abingdon, 1968, p. 9.

smaller proportion of the total number of students than was the case in the nineteenth century. These colleges also play a far less influential role in the whole of American higher education than was the case a hundred years ago. They often appear to be following the examples set by state colleges and universities rather than leading. The purposes for which they were founded no longer seem to be guiding them, and often no clear direction can be seen in their educational processes. Merrimon Cuninggim puts the matter succinctly: "Protestant efforts in higher education are in a state of considerable disrepair." [3]

Though the primary focus here is the Protestant college, most of what is said has wider application. Roman Catholic higher education, if the turmoil within it may be taken as evidence of its condition, is confronted with similar problems. At the 1967 commencement of St. Mary's College, the Very Reverend Charles S. Casassa, S.J., president of Loyola University of Los Angeles, spoke of the difficult problems confronting Catholic institutions. After pointing to the "sad fact" that Catholic colleges and universities have "multiplied enormously" in the past twenty-five years, he added: "Weak, understaffed, thinly spread, poor in resources and quality, many of these institutions are really diluted Catholic higher education. We could stand some kind of intellectual pill to regulate proliferation of such institutions." [4] Perhaps our prescription in what follows will help both to retard meaningless births and to make surviving colleges healthier.

The widespread concern and unease over that portion of higher education sponsored by churches takes many forms. In part it is concern over quality. A few church-related colleges and universities are in the forefront. But, if one were to adopt David Riesman's figure of higher education as "a snake-like procession," then most of the institutions under church auspices are in the sluggish middle or back toward the tail. In part, it is concern over the increasing difficulties of financing them and securing adequate administrative leadership. Those with an interest in church-related colleges know what James

---

[3] Merrimon Cuninggim, *The Protestant Stake in Higher Education.* Washington: Council of Protestant Colleges and Universities, 1961, p. 30.

[4] Reported in the *San Francisco Sunday Examiner and Chronicle,* June 11, 1967, p. 12. See also Robert Hassenger (ed.), *The Shape of Catholic Higher Education.* Chicago: University of Chicago Press, 1967.

B. Angell said clearly in 1871 is even more true today: "In this day of unparalleled activity in college life, the institution which is not steadily advancing is certainly falling behind." [5] But the basic concern is probably over purpose. What is the place of the church-related college in this "age of the university," when higher education in this country is dominated by state-supported institutions and only the few private and church-related schools that are rich in prestige and endowment can maintain the pace?

The painful fact is that church-related colleges of all denominations have been undergoing important but inadequately noted changes in their internal structure, in their constituencies, in their patterns of funding, and in the purposes for which they are operated. The basic rethinking of the nature and meaning that these changes make necessary has not been taking place among the leadership of most of these institutions. As a consequence, despite many encouraging signs, there is developing an ominous set of symptoms: an overall sense of uncertainty on many campuses that threatens to degenerate into opportunism; a confusion in regard to basic direction that often approaches drift; and growing anxiety that often verges on a loss of nerve. In spite of these symptoms and the genuine problems underlying them, there is substantial basis for controlled optimism. But it must be based on careful analysis and realistic action.

3. Historical Illusion and Reality

If one glances at the new buildings going up, the recent rise in faculty salaries, and the confident look in the president's eye as he addresses public gatherings, there would seem to be no reason for alarm over the resurrected church college. But those who give more attention to the situation behind the scenes know all is not well. To understand what may appear as contradictory elements in the present situation, a look into the background and development of the church-related colleges is necessary.

Franklin Littell has said that "the major problem before the churches in America is the achievement of self-understanding." No small part of self-understanding is an adequate view of the past; and in few areas are Christians plagued by more misunderstanding

---

[5] Quoted in Frederick Rudolph, *The American College: A History.* New York: Knopf, 1962, p. 329.

than with reference to the history of American higher education and the place of religion in our educational heritage. The prevailing view about that past can only be evaluated as pernicious because it offers illusions as to where church colleges have come from and hence as to the present in which they must respond and the future they may realistically anticipate. Donald G. Tewksbury comments on the "errors of fact and interpretation" occurring in catalogs and college histories that are transferred to general works and accepted as authoritative.[6]

It is said often that higher education in the United States is the child of religion. This is probably true of the British colonies if one means that the founders of the early colleges were also active churchmen and Christian believers and that they assumed their continuity with the learning of European Christendom. Brubacher and Rudy are correct in saying that "the Christian tradition was the foundation stone of the whole intellectual structure which was brought to the New World." [7] But it is often mistakenly assumed on the basis of the religious roots of the colonial colleges that the church-related campus of today stands in direct continuity with the colonial heritage that provided the foundation for our system of higher education. This is not precisely the case.

The colleges of the colonial period were the product of a societal effort to serve the welfare of the whole community. They were not, in the later sense of the term, church colleges. Frederick Rudolph writes: "Harvard, William and Mary, and Yale . . . were creatures as much of the state as of the established churches. . . . And whether they should be thought of as state colleges or as church colleges is a problem in semantics that is perhaps best resolved by calling them state-church colleges." [8] It would be better still to call them *public Christian colleges*. They were founded for the public interest as then conceived, to serve the common good, and to provide civic leaders capable of coping with the societal problems of the time. They were not founded to serve special interests but rather the purposes of the commonwealth. From the vantage point of the twentieth century, colonial societies appear narrow in scope. Nonetheless, colleges were

---

[6] Donald G. Tewksbury, *The Founding of American Colleges and Universities before the Civil War.* New York: Anchor Books, 1932, p. 29.

[7] Brubacher and Rudy, op. cit., p. 6.

[8] Rudolph, op. cit., p. 13.

intended to serve the entire community, not a special segment. In their founding and in their support, they were both public and Christian, but not church-related in the nineteenth- and twentieth-century meaning.

The church-related colleges of today are not in direct continuity with the public Christian colleges of the colonial era. Private and state-supported colleges and universities are the heirs of prerevolutionary public Christian higher education, becoming at first non-denominationally Protestant and then pluralistically religious as the societal climate shifted. Our present-day colleges, which are or have been until recently related to ecclesiastical bodies, derive from the proliferation of sectarian colleges in the nineteenth century. These colleges emerged only indirectly from the impetus of colonial higher education and most directly from the revivalistic impulses seeking to convert and tame the frontier. With notable exceptions, they were founded primarily to serve the purposes of a denominational constituency as these goals mingled with the interests of particular localities and ethnic groupings. They were controlled in doctrine, moral precepts, and social outlook by sectarian views and were designed in large measure to protect students from the "dangers" of other educational environments and to inculcate the faith and morals acceptable to their constituency. To this end, they were usually local in focus and isolated from general societal influences. While the language of the founders and early presidents might sound loftier themes, these colleges functioned in quite limited spheres. Even as they played an important role in bringing a modicum of culture and civilizing influence to the American frontier, it is not difficult to see them as fostering an anti-intellectual climate in keeping with the emotional emphases of revivalism and contributing to a dissolution of the educational criteria developed by the colonial colleges of the Eastern Seaboard. Only gradually did the pressures of survival force the sectarian colleges of the nineteenth century to expand the horizons of potential students, to give greater attention to academic excellence than to doctrinal and moral rectitude, and to enter the larger public context of colonial higher education and the institutions that followed its example.

But not all did survive. The mortality rate for the sectarian colleges that proliferated without plan or control throughout the nineteenth and early twentieth centuries was high—higher probably among Roman Catholic colleges than among Protestant institutions. Tewksbury reports that only 145 Protestant colleges of a probable total exceeding 700 founded before 1865 survived until 1929, indicating the heavy mortality rate among sectarian establishments. The church-related colleges of today are those that have managed to stay alive, survivors under some as-yet-undefined law of fitness. In suggesting that survival was not wholly a matter of natural selection, Jencks and Riesman write:

> Colleges founded to preserve a particular kind of orthodoxy had a much lower life expectancy than colleges whose founders possessed a more expansive and more academic view of their role. . . . Many Protestant colleges have [changed], starting with sectarian ties that were ill-adapted to market conditions and deciding (often unconsciously) as time went on to play these ties down and in some cases eventually eliminating them.[9]

The colleges that could adapt have survived into an era when the state and federal governments have entered into higher education on a massive scale. Increasingly the sectarian past has run afoul of the public present. The alternative has been to become more public or to perish.

The problem is not that of having a sectarian past. Rather it is when this past is perceived through a haze of romanticism and self-justification that change to meet a new situation becomes difficult. The public present is painfully visible to the envious ecclesiastical eye. But will church-related colleges have the freedom and insight to respond? This is the dilemma now confronting them. And behind the varied and insistent forms that the dilemma of sectarian past vs. public present assumes, there is a basic, all-pervading issue, one with social, educational, and theological dimensions.

4. Hard Facts and Difficult Questions

The evidence is widespread and convincing that the church-related college, despite improvement on many fronts in recent years, faces continuing problems that cannot be overcome by sporadic infusions of federal green. James A. Perkins speaks of the paradox of the modern university as "dangerously close to becoming the victim of its own

---

[9] Christopher Jencks and David Riesman, *The Academic Revolution*. Garden City, New York: Doubleday, 1968, p. 327.

success." But this paradox of problem and plenty is not an adequate way to characterize the difficulties confronting church-related colleges. Though there is an upper crust that is relatively secure, most denominational colleges are plagued by a persistently dangerous situation. The problems center in the areas of governance and finance. And many colleges continue on the verge of catastrophe, even though conditions appear vastly better as compared with three or even two decades ago. It is a paradox of precarious affluence.

Clearly, the problems of church-related higher education do not derive from flood conditions but from prolonged drought—in regard to adequate leadership, quality teaching staff, top-flight students, and funds to meet increasing operating costs—a drought not overcome by gifts and loans for buildings. The shortage of operating funds appears to hard-pressed presidents and trustees as the most urgent problem. But budgetary deficits may well derive from a nexus of other deficiencies, e.g., failure to uncover new sources of support may be caused by unimaginative administrative leadership.

Many assume that the basic issue for the church-related college is *survival*. Scores of sectarian colleges begun in the nineteenth and early twentieth centuries do not exist today. When one remembers the high mortality rate in the past, the rising operational costs today, and the vast reservoir of public funds devoted to higher education, there is considerable cogency in defining the problem in the simple terms of survival. But that is merely where the deeper problems culminate, where they pinch most painfully. Behind the issue of survival lies a congeries of hard facts and difficult questions that must be faced, adding up to a dilemma pressing irresistibly upon church-sponsored higher education.

For the colleges that have managed to survive, the past half century has been a time of testing and transition. The church-related and private sectors of higher education have decreased dramatically in relation to the public sector. In 1900, of the 240,000 students in institutions of higher education, four out of every five attended a church-related or private college. Today, with enrollment in American higher education approximating eight million, around three of every four students attend public institutions, and in the huge California system of higher education, the 1900 ratio has already reversed itself. The nonpublic institutions that have done well are mostly a handful of prestigious private colleges and universities.

Most church-related institutions have had a long, uphill struggle. Certain of them are probably superfluous, and many must undergo radical change or be closed.

Among the realities to be faced is that of the generally lower overall quality of the church-related institutions. A few are good, but most fall in the lower or middle range of the quality spectrum. For example, of the 49 institutions, 34 universities, and 15 colleges that produced 25 or more Woodrow Wilson Fellows in the period 1945-60, only 3 universities (Notre Dame, Northwestern, and Duke) and 3 colleges (Swarthmore, Haverford, and Kenyon) can be regarded as church-related. Of 32 institutions that produced 15 to 24 Woodrow Wilson Fellows in the same period, only 8 are related to churches (Davidson, Fordham, Occidental, St. Louis, Emory, University of the South, Grinnell, and Beloit). Of a total of 81, only 14 are church-related,[10] and it must be confessed few of these are closely affiliated with churches. One may argue with some justice that the academic achievement and prestige measured by the number of Woodrow Wilson Fellowships are not the only criteria to apply, but this excuse does not alter the hard fact that church-sponsored institutions do not rank high on the scale of general academic excellence.

Along with mediocre quality is the problem of inadequate leadership. Caught in the patterns of selection coming from the sectarian past, the church-related college has drawn its leadership for administrative and policy posts from the ranks of successful clergymen, pastors, devoted laymen, and persons trained primarily in theology. These persons have given themselves unstintingly for the most part, and a few have adapted superbly. Overall, however, they have not been able to cope sufficiently with the rapidly changing context of contemporary education to overcome the quality gap. They have proved inadequate for an era when higher education has become increasingly oriented toward public purposes and research, and must recruit its students and faculty and finance itself from other than ecclesiastical sources. Lacking educational vision and know-how to meet contemporary demands, these men have usually been able to hold the institution together but not to develop it creatively. An

---

[10] Manning M. Pattillo, Jr., and Donald M. Mackenzie, *Church-Sponsored Higher Education in the United States: Report of the Danforth Commission.* Washington, 1966, pp. 117-120.

encouraging sign today on the church-related scene is the increasing tendency to look beyond the traditional boundaries for new leadership.

The complaint that the church-related college is unable to get and hold good faculty members attributes the blame most often to the relatively poor pay scale. It has probably been true, however, that teaching at the church-related college has been better than the salaries because at each one there is a small core of professors dedicated to the traditions and educational goals of the college. Not all faculty members are intent on advancing their careers by moving to large, well-financed universities. Many like the setting of a smaller college without the intense pressures toward research and publishing present in major academic centers. The issue is often whether younger faculty feel themselves in tune with the purposes of the college and whether they believe something significant educationally is going on. It is possible that administrative leadership with a vision appropriate for contemporary education would be able not only to hold more good faculty members but also to raise more money to pay them better. In any event, it is clear that higher salaries alone will not solve the problem of improving instruction, whether there is a shortage or excess of qualified teachers for our expanding higher education.

In addition, there are other problems relating to quality of instruction. The isolated situation of these institutions makes it more difficult to supplement classroom instruction with cultural events, field trips, etc. This problem is intensified when it is recognized that education today must be related to the urban context of American life. Or again, small and medium-sized colleges have tended to reproduce the pattern of academic disciplines within the university, leading to small, inadequately staffed departments. Library resources have often been poor, a situation that makes high-quality instruction, even with an excellent faculty, difficult, if not impossible. On another count, the patterns of self-selection on the part of students who decide to attend these colleges have often been other than intellectual. For a high academic level, it is necessary to have excellent students, and the denominational colleges have not, on the average, been drawing them. Still further, the heavy class load as well as these other problems, often discourages promising teachers from coming or remaining.

In the light of these many difficulties, the thorny issue of finances must be examined. Though the financial situation of the church-related college has been improving over the past two decades, the rate and bases of this improvement leave room for much concern and questioning. Faculty salaries are better, but a recent American Association of University Professors report listing 275 colleges and universities with faculty salaries averaging $10,000 or more contains few church-related institutions. The rate of improvement has not been keeping pace with the increasing national average. Many new buildings have been placed alongside the decrepit ivy-covered ones over the past fifteen years, but high indebtedness related to these facilities suggests an increasingly precarious financial position. The growing dependence on student tuition and fees for the rising operating budget of the college necessitates recruiting from higher-income groups. The resultant snob appeal and reinforcement of class patterns may give temporary aid on the problem of money but places the church-related college in a highly dubious position with regard to the professed social aims of the Christian community. The increased availability and acceptance of grants and loans from the federal government, a relatively new feature of the church-related scene that does much to explain recent building programs, have undoubtedly solved certain financial problems. But the presence of federal financing only underscores the tension within church-sponsored higher education between its sectarian past and its public present.

Underlying all these problems is the lack of personnel and facilities for careful research and planning as the basis for policy decisions on the part of church colleges and, what is even more serious, a general unawareness that such policy planning is important. Unable to do the task individually, it will be necessary for colleges to develop policy staffs on a cooperative basis or for some agency to take on the task for them.

Whether one views these problems with alarm or surveys these developments with satisfaction, the issues for the denominational college today extend beyond the simple one of survival. Pressures from many directions are putting stress upon the entire fabric of these schools as they relate to the churches, their constituencies, and the society around them. The following questions must be faced, and the answers will not come easily.

What is the crucial problem confronting denominational colleges

30

today? Given the context and direction of higher education in the United States, can colleges find a way in which to be uniquely Christian? Within the ecumenical and pluralistic culture of America and the world, does a place exist for church-related higher education? What role can denominational colleges play today in a scene increasingly dominated by public higher education? Are there tasks in the educational process to which church-related higher education may make important contributions? What is the future of the church-sponsored college, and in what directions will it be moving? It seems increasingly clear that a time of agonizing reappraisal has arrived—reappraisal on the part of colleges traditionally related to churches; reappraisal on the part of the denominational bodies sponsoring these colleges. Some of this rethinking is already under way, but it must become more searching and realistic than ever before.

Chapter II

CRISIS OF IDENTITY

DESPITE THE RISE to dominance of the graduate schools and the massive shift toward public higher education in this century, church-related colleges have confounded the prophets of doom and refused to die. What is more, a surprising number have actually been thriving, with increased enrollments, higher faculty salaries, new buildings, and, not infrequently, improved academic performance. While their financial structure is often precarious, these colleges have been surviving and even bettering their position in the academic marketplace.

With this recent history in mind, it becomes possible to envision a future for the old Christian college in its resurrected form. Perhaps there is after all a need for these colleges that sprang from sectarian roots and have managed to endure in a dry and rocky academic environment. But not all have survived and not all presently in operation will continue. The expansion of the states into the community college sphere will endanger further the already precarious existence of scores of denominational colleges in all parts of the nation, as also will economic recession and inflation.

For any college—public, private, or church-related—to make its way today, there must be careful facing of hard problems, expert projection of alternative futures, and bold pursuit of policies selected. Lessons must be learned from past failures and successes, not merely within the experience of one college and its leadership but from the widest range of data that can be obtained. The era of leadership that relied primarily on snap judgment and personal charisma is over. Church-related colleges have learned this lesson too slowly, but it has been taking hold. Leadership today must include resources for a comprehensive information system, expert analysis of problems, and the development of policy alternatives, as well as the ability to make decisions firmly and to persuade vigorously.

Given these needs, it is amazing how little careful research has been done on church-related colleges. No comprehensive history of the churches and higher education in the United States exists, and little of the material on particular colleges or areas of interest has given sufficient attention to the social and political context to make it useful to policy-makers in denominational colleges. Thanks to the Danforth Foundation a study of church-sponsored higher education was undertaken in 1962. The report of this study[1] provides an important initial reservoir of information about the colleges conducted under church auspices. For example, we learn that in 1962-63, there were 817 colleges and universities that could be considered church-sponsored, quite a sizable percentage of the institutions of higher education in the nation. Other basic data about geographic distribution, students, relationship to church bodies, trustees, income, curriculum, libraries, etc., are provided. But the Danforth study offers only a beginning.

Now it is necessary to go further and pinpoint in more detail the central problems of church-related colleges, delineate dangerous directions of movement, and project productive alternatives.

1. Sectarian Past and Public Present in Conflict

The central dilemma of the church-related college can be expressed most accurately as follows: it is caught between its sectarian past and its public present. It would be a misunderstanding of this dilemma, as well as an inaccurate appraisal of the present situation, to think it means that church-sponsored higher education is dominated today by sectarianism. The old Christian college is no more, if one ignores

---

[1] Manning M. Pattillo, Jr., and Donald M. Mackenzie, *Church-Sponsored Higher Education in the United States: Report of the Danforth Commission.* Washington, 1966. See also the following helpful studies: Guy E. Snavely, *The Church and the Four-Year College.* New York: Harper, 1955. Myron F. Wicke, *The Church-Related College.* Washington: Center for Applied Research in Education, 1964.

a few anachronistic examples that have managed to maintain a pseudo-nineteenth-century climate by means of slick twentieth-century appeals to a nostalgic constituency. Church-related colleges exist in the public present, but the pull of their sectarian past creates problems.

Some would deny their sectarian origins. And quotations from founders and presidents can be found that have an expansive ring and would seem to contradict beginnings at the hands of special-interest groups. These statements then, no doubt, had much the same rhetorical import and utility that similar statements in catalogs and on public occasions have today. In their actual operations, denominationally sponsored colleges of the nineteenth century fit the sectarian mold quite well. Perhaps the ecumenical rhetoric of leading churchmen and the denominational imperialism of their churches in recent decades provide the best current analogy. Most church-related colleges remaining today stand in continuity with this sectarian past.

In this century, there has been a growing reaction against sectarianism in higher education. The tendency is illustrated by the movement of many colleges away from denominational control and affiliation and by the tremendous growth in the public sector of higher education. The reaction is also clear within colleges still related to ecclesiastical bodies. Churchmen with educational vision, both lay and clergy, have opposed sectarian strictures on curriculum and educational processes. The movement has been even more decisive, though by no means unanimous, among faculty and students. But apart from vision or sentiment, the realities of the evolving educational context have forced changes. To secure competent faculty, able students, and adequate financing, church-related colleges have been compelled increasingly to phase out sectarian emphases and to imitate public and private colleges. This process began in most sectarian colleges soon after they were founded, and the momentum of the change has increased. Pattillo and Mackenzie report that only a "loose, vaguely defined religion" is reflected on the campuses of many church-related colleges today. And they are quite correct in concluding: "People who think that rigid sectarianism is the principal defect of church-related higher education are fifty years behind the times." [2]

---

[2] Pattillo and Mackenzie, op. cit., p. 88.

Within the emerging public style, however, the sectarian past still exerts considerable power. The tension produced by this conflict needs examination in order to learn how to cope with it productively.

Viewed from one standpoint, the "special-interest" origin of these colleges still exercises, to greater and lesser degrees in specific instances, much control over the self-understanding and operational patterns of those responsible for policy formation and personnel selection. Seen in a different perspective, these colleges find themselves changing in response to demands from local communities, from constituencies of varied denominational and economic interests, from students of diverse backgrounds, from academic accrediting agencies, and from governmental sources of money.

No single statement of the conflict between past and present will describe all church-related colleges. A few have adjusted to the present so well that little tension can be discerned. Others attempt, with varying degrees of success, to lead a schizophrenic existence in which trustees and ecclesiastical constituencies are kept in ignorance of the accommodation of student life, faculty selection, and academic style to current trends in higher education. Another group appeals to conservative religious constituencies on an interdenominational rather than a sectarian basis. Only a small group continues to represent the sectarian collegiate pattern that was general in the late nineteenth century.

The first of these groups has, for the most part, overcome the tension. Indeed, many have loosened or discarded church ties. The latter two groups appeal to the still significant constituency that prefers doctrinal orthodoxy (however conceived) and strict moral controls to academic excellence and wider educational horizons. None of these groups feels with intensity the press of conflict between past and present.

It is the colleges caught in the middle for which the tension between past and present is powerful and the problem elevated into agonizing awareness. For this group, a discussion of the central dilemma of church-related colleges may prove illuminating and helpful.

Many aspects of these colleges reflect the continuing grip of their sectarian past in tension with the demands of their public present. The rhetoric of statements prepared for ecclesiastical bodies and church-oriented parents stands in sharp contrast to descriptions of the college provided for accrediting associations, government agencies, or charitable foundations. The catalog will probably combine both in lofty professions of high academic purpose and profound character development. In the pattern of choosing trustees, the sectarian past will be mingled with a shrewd sense of where the money is. In the selection of faculty, only a reluctance to appoint militant atheists will betray earlier doctrinal criteria. The one important exception is in the appointment of faculty who will teach courses in religion. Here the sectarian past still triumphs, though the ecumenical movement shows some limited influence. Choice of presidents and deans presents a scene of mixed and often covert criteria, which offer at the moment probably the best clue as to the location of a college on the spectrum of past and present.

When one examines the expectations of the college held by its oldest, strongest, and perhaps its wealthiest supporters, the statement on religion in the catalog, and the residence hall regulations still in force or recently modified, the church-related college looks more like the nineteenth-century institution it was founded to be. When one looks at its present sources of funds, at faculty and curriculum, at campus life, and at the college bookstore, it appears as a somewhat less affluent and less exciting version of its public and private counterparts.

At no point in the present existence of church-related colleges is the conflict sharper than in the program of religious activities. Here there has been a general attempt to hold to remnants of the sectarian past longer and more tenaciously than at any other point. Academic program, admissions policies, and funding sources can be changed to meet the demands of the public present, but religious activities must serve to reassure the constituencies oriented toward the sectarian past. Unhappily, these religious programs held over from the past have encountered students straining toward the future and have been staffed by younger clergy who are reacting against sectarian religion and the social conservatism that usually accompanies it. The result has ranged from conflict to catastrophe. The campus minister and his activist students have proved painful embarrassments to the president as he faces trustees, community leaders, and wealthy donors. And the college has been no less an embarrassment to the campus minister as he seeks to develop student and faculty involvement in Christian reflection and action. It is the stuff from which tragic dramas could be derived if directed at the feelings and lives of those immediately involved and from which may come musical comedies when the events are overlaid with the romantic haze of a few decades.

The contrast is illumined further when one examines higher education historically rather than at the present moment in isolation. The criterion of usefulness to society was not first introduced by Benjamin Franklin and Thomas Jefferson, as James A. Perkins suggests. The public Christian colleges of the colonial period were shaped by their utility for the community that founded them. The nineteenth century, following Franklin and Jefferson, widened the areas of use to which higher education would be put, developing research and training to serve the practical purposes of agriculture and industry, purposes expanded and given further definition as the result of the Federal Land Grant Act of 1862. Public and private higher education in the nineteenth century continued the heritage of the colonial colleges in that they were founded for the public interest, served the common good of the larger community, and were involved with society and its problems. Close relation to societal interests meant immediate relevance to the needs of articulate and powerful sectors. Upon the basis of this service, the increasing budgets from public sources for the entire educational enterprise were built. But the ability to criticize the purposes and priorities of the society became more problematic as reliance on public approval grew.

The church-related colleges of today did not emerge from this tradition of public usefulness but rather within the context of sectarian competition and expansionist revivalism. Though some leaders gave voice to wide humanitarian aspirations and a few colleges did not fit the sectarian image, most were established to serve special groups with limited scope and purpose, defined most usually by denomination and immediate region. They were defensive in regard to the sectarian, regional convictions that nurtured them. The purposes and operation of these colleges were designed to protect students from the dangers of worldliness and indoctrinate them in the correct version of Christian faith. The sectarian college was usually isolated by intention of its founders, one being located, according to a report, forty miles from any known form of sin.

In their style of operation and instruction, in the shape of their constituencies, church-related colleges have, through imitation of public and private institutions, joined the tradition of the public Christian colleges of the colonial period and the utilitarian public education that developed in the nineteenth century. To a considerable degree, however, the church-related college has held onto a sectarian ideology that speaks to its traditions and older constituencies. The transition into the newer public style has produced much stress, but the need for maintaining vestiges of sectarianism has compounded stress with confusion.

When the situation of church-related higher education is put in this way, one suspects that the principal problem is not survival nor quality nor finances but rather is a *crisis of identity* in the individual institutions, a crisis that reflects a larger uncertainty within the churches. On the one hand, there is a widespread tendency to repudiate the sectarian past, often without trying to salvage what may be worth retaining. And on the other hand, there is a furious effort to catch up with a rapidly changing order, as if relevance to society were alone sufficient. One can almost hear the pathetic cry from desperate churchmen, "Please stop the world—we want to get on!"

2. Role, Purpose, and Identity

Out of the dilemma occasioned by the tension between sectarian past and public present emerges a crisis of identity for church-related colleges. To understand this crisis, we must explore what it means to speak of institutional identity, elaborate in greater detail the nature of the identity crisis within these colleges, and suggest ways in which the crisis can be resolved.

Though much that has been written about the identity crisis focuses on the psychological growth of individual persons, the concept applies to social entities such as movements, institutions, and nations. Indeed, it is doubtful that an identity crisis has significance for an individual save as he is a social entity with a communally shared past, relations to others in the present involving mutual expectations and interacting roles, and common purposes that point toward an anticipated future. A sense of identity means that the disparate strands of experience are held together in a sufficiently coherent fashion as to provide a basis for action, action responsive to real relations to others and the real expectations others have.

Whether it be an individual, a group, an institution, a society, or a nation, an identity adequate for action is an essential for the entity to function. And a meaningful sense of identity is crucial for healthy functioning.

Erikson speaks of a sense of identity as "the accrued confidence that the inner sameness and continuity are matched by the sameness and continuity of one's meaning for others, as evidenced in the tangible promise of a career." [3] He contrasts identity with role diffusion, which threatens a loss of identity and produces an identity crisis.

Quite clearly such an understanding can be applied to those selves embodied in what we call institutions and social entities as well as to what we call individual persons. Erikson makes this application. He suggests that "a nation's identity is derived from the ways in which history has, as it were, counterpointed certain opposite potentialities; the ways in which it lifts this counterpoint to a unique style of civilization, or lets it disintegrate into mere contradiction." [4]

A sense of identity for all social and historical selves derives from the ability to place the past, with its commitments, actions, and structured responses, into continuity with the roles and functions the present calls forth and with the purposes and expectations that are the meaningful presence of the future. When present and past are in conflict, when the functions demanded in the present appear incompatible, and when possibilities cannot be integrated into a career projecting into the future, then there is a situation of role diffusion and identity crisis. Surely this description applies to many institutions of higher education today and with special force to that marginal group, the church-related colleges.

For the denominational college the purposes it finds itself serving today and the roles it is committed to fulfill are often in conflict precisely because of the disparity between the commitments that informed its past and the demands of its present. Those colleges that have not resolved these tensions in some relatively satisfactory manner are undergoing a crisis of identity.

The past of most church-related colleges contains many elements difficult to combine with the present. This past is not gone but remains in the vivid memories of many members of controlling and funding bodies, as well as being embodied in institutional pat-

---

[3] Erik H. Erikson, *Childhood and Society*. New York: Norton, 1950, p. 261.
[4] *Ibid.*, p. 285.

terns. Past commitments to the founding denomination remain powerful in the present through methods for choosing trustees and administrators, in the methods for recruiting faculty and students, in the constituencies to which appeals for funds are made, and in many campus regulations—those governing compulsory chapel, residence hall rules, and student behavior.

Many demands of the present, however, are in conflict with this continuing past. The ecumenical spirit of our time has brought into question restrictive patterns of worship, moralistic rules, and denominational requirements for administration and faculty deriving from the sectarian past. Denominational sources of financing have declined relative to the needs of today's college, and sources of funding are opening up that require the disavowal of sectarianism. Faculty recruitment must be done on the basis of academic competence rather than on church loyalty. And prospective students are not attracted so much as in the past by denominational labels, even those coming from the church that has been the traditional sponsor of the college.

The purposes the college serves must be enunciated to newer and younger constituencies in ways that violate the expectations of more traditional constituencies. The functions the college is called upon to perform in the present do not square easily with those of the past, and the institutional patterns shaped by the past often work poorly today. The divergent demands of the present and the projections required in planning for the future are not only filled with difficulties in themselves, but these problems are compounded by institutional patterns and expectations held over from the past. This conflict among past, present, and future makes the task of developing a viable identity appear at times impossible. Small wonder that the only solution some colleges have found is the isolation of different constituencies from one another, the presentation of different institutional images to each, and the action calculated to prevent the various groups from comparing notes.

3. Images and Constituencies

Clark Kerr has said that college presidents are often accused of being two-faced. He replies that this charge is patently false. No president, Kerr contends, can survive by being merely two-faced; he must present many faces to the various constituencies he confronts—

the trustees, the funding bodies, the faculty, the students, the alumni, the parents, and the general public. Clearly this is the case not only for the college president but for the institution itself. And nowhere is this multifaceted need more vividly illustrated than in the church-related college.

For better or worse, various groups to which the college is related have different conceptions of what an institution ought to be doing and indeed what it is doing. Administrators and public-relations departments expend time and energy in cultivating different constituencies and presenting images to these groups that will elicit their support. The president and his corps of administrators interpret the work of the college to the trustees, to bodies that select the controlling board, to groups and individuals who supply funds, to the surrounding community, to present and potential faculty members, to prospective students, and to the present student body. At times administrators and others may be asked to explain the actions of one of these groups to another and it is hoped to convince the constituency being addressed that its own image of the college is not incompatible with the actions of the former group. This task of interpretation is not always easy. When a faculty member takes an unpopular public stand or students engage in a public demonstration against war, the trustees and funding bodies may wonder whether their image of the college is being fulfilled. On the other hand, when the trustees reaffirm a policy of compulsory chapel or rigid residence hall regulations, the students and many of the faculty may wonder whether they wish to be part of such an institution. The more disparate the images held by different constituencies, the more difficult it becomes to interpret one to the other and the greater danger that the efforts at interpretation will result in a credibility gap and loss of confidence rather than in continuing support.

Such is the composition of the role diffusion from which emerges the crisis of identity for many colleges—church-related, private, and public. Divergent images are held by different constituencies, images leading to differing expectations concerning the purposes the college serves, the policies to be adopted, the behavior to be expected on the part of persons and groups making up the college, and the appropriate responses when images come into conflict.

Some confirmed optimists hold resolutely to the notion that better communication among various constituencies will produce better understanding and that improved understanding will inevitably lead to greater peace, cooperation, and progress. Much of the turmoil on campuses today undoubtedly results from better communication. Students have more information about the administration and trustees and about the social meaning of the policies pursued by these groups. It is equally clear that presidents, deans, and board members are much aware of the national and global scope of student activism—and are much more nervous and wary as a consequence. Students on each campus know about the widespread incidence of student rebellion, thanks to the mass media, and student activists have developed less public means of communication to learn from one another and coordinate their actions. Better communication has certainly not increased understanding. And, when one becomes optimistic about the uses of improved understanding, he is reminded of G. K. Chesterton's story, which begins by saying that two men understood each other so well that naturally one of them had to kill the other.

The identity crisis will be solved, not by ignoring the chasms between constituencies produced by differing images, but rather by giving careful attention to the variety and developing interpretations of the colleges that include the diversity and on this basis provide for operational unity.

4. Toward Solving the Identity Crisis

All problems of identity have elements in common. Role misunderstanding, produced by the conflict between past and future and the contradictory function demanded by the present, is central to every identity crisis, whether in the life of the individual person, institutional community, or nation. There are also aspects that vary, not only from lesser to more comprehensive social entities, but also from instance to instance, just as each person differs from every other and particular groups and institutions differ in crucial ways even from similar entities of about the same purpose and form. We cannot hope here to do more than point out productive directions for understanding and action in solving the identity problems of a specific college.

Still further, identity crises are not overcome by analysis and understanding exclusively. These procedures may lead to recognition of the dilemma and to rational comprehension of possible solutions.

42

But life is more encompassing than reason, however broadly conceived. Real living is acting, meeting, responding with believing, reflecting, evaluating as a constant accompaniment.

The resolution of identity crises must be achieved within the process of human living. This is no less true for institutional communities than for persons. From one viewpoint it may be seen as akin to psychotherapy, in which insight is gained, relationships healed, integration of conflicting roles and purposes achieved, and new styles of action developed. From another perspective it may be seen as political process in which alternative purposes and policies are clarified, wider conceptions developed that represent interests previously thought to be opposed, power relations adjusted to new social realities, and a community of authority welded together that permits functioning unity while allowing for continuing and creative diversity.

For these reasons resolving the crisis of identity in a church-related college, or in any social entity, cannot be effected at a distance. Only those closely involved with the specific complexities and commitments existing in a community can see the real alternatives and command the loyalties that will promote wholeness and a sense of identity sufficient for corporate action. Such resolution certainly cannot be provided in a book. But it may be possible to offer viewpoints that will aid in diagnosing institutional illness, delineate pathological syndromes, and suggest therapeutic and politically feasible directions for study and action.

We have already pointed in various ways to the problems that plague denominationally sponsored institutions of higher education and described the core of the difficulties as an identity crisis occasioned by the role diffusion resulting from the tension between sectarian past and public present. Now we must move further to specify elements in this crisis and alternatives to be explored in order to resolve it.

Chapter III

THE QUEST FOR UNIQUENESS

IN CONCLUDING their study of church-sponsored higher education, Pattillo and Mackenzie write: "Church institutions sorely need models of their own to serve as broad conceptual frameworks." [1] No single model will suffice, for there is no single right answer to the question, "What is a Christian college?" This was not always the case. The General Conference of the Methodist Episcopal Church in 1824 put the matter in direct and simple terms: "The Christian College is the bulwark of the Christian Church." [2] This statement was quoted with approval in the catalog of at least one denominational college as late as 1927. In 1832, the Indiana Methodist Conference put the matter in this delicate form:

> When we examine the state of the literary institutions of our country, we find a majority of them are in the hands of other denominations, so that our people are unwilling (and we think properly so) to send their sons to those institutions. Therefore we think it very desirable to have an institution under our own control from which we can exclude all doctrines which we deem dangerous; though at the same time we do not wish to make it so sectarian as to exclude or in the smallest degree repel the sons of our fellow citizens from the same. [3]

Tewksbury points out, "Colleges came in many cases to be regarded as agents of a type of denominational imperialism, and as a means

---

[1] Op. cit., p. 213.
[2] Quoted in Tewksbury, op. cit., p. 55.
[3] William Warren Sweet, *Indiana Asbury-Depauw University, 1837-1937*. Nashville: Abingdon Press, 1937, p. 26. Quoted in Rudolph, op. cit., p. 56.

of sectarian aggrandizement and aggression," with higher education as an arena of intense competition and conflict among the churches.[4]

The ecclesiastical and sectarian views of the nineteenth century are no longer viable. But what models should replace them are not always clear. As leaders of church colleges seek guidelines to set policies and project images of the enterprise to various constituencies, they reach in many directions, not all of them fruitful. One of the most pervasive and pernicious images to be found today in denominational colleges undergoing a crisis of identity is that of uniqueness.

1. The Persistent Question

Rather than seeing the problem as that of a sectarian past versus a public present, many leaders of church colleges view the dilemma as distinctive past versus isomorphic present. The denominational college once had distinctive purposes and roles. Even though it might have existed primarily for a limited clientele, its Christian purposes gave it universal meaning and its sectarian shape gave it unique resources to serve these wider goals. Today many educators see most colleges, public and nonpublic, moving toward a deadly sameness, an amorphous sterility. For these leaders, the peril is isomorphism, the mutual imitation among institutions that robs them of distinctiveness.

Much can be said in support of this point of view. The sectarian college, whatever else may be said about it, bore the stamp of denominational control in its faculty and curriculum, in its board of trustees and administrative leadership, in its patterns of worship and campus rules, in its students and their escapades, and even in the areas in which it chose to relate itself to society. Today the church-related college often tries so hard to imitate state and private schools in its faculty, instructional program, and campus life as to present a picture of bland isomorphism. Some institutions have resolved the tension between past and present by cutting all denominational ties and attempting to jettison their religious tradition. Others have retained only tenuous relations and for all practical purposes have ceased to operate within the context of faith in which they were founded. But a substantial number of colleges still wrestle with the tension between past and present. For leaders of these colleges a

---

[4] Op. cit., p. 213.

persistent question is: What is the unique function of the Christian college? [5]

Though variously phrased and no longer having the narrower overtones of the nineteenth century, the question asks for a reply indicating some activity, some function or functions, the church-related college can perform that will set it apart from a public or private institution. What is the special thing, or things, a college sponsored by religious groups can do that those not so sponsored cannot do?

This question is a pressing one for many college administrators and faculty, and for trustees and church officials concerned about the present and the future of denominational colleges. Should ties to denominations be continued if there is nothing of great distinctiveness to be gained for the churches, for the colleges, or for human society? Surely Christian faith and elements in the educational environment derived from it offer not only a distinctive but a unique contribution that cannot be duplicated by non-Christian institutions. Many arguments beginning with or assuming such a view as this are made by those committed to the continuation of this or that denominational college.

From one standpoint, the quest for uniqueness can be seen as the persistence in more covert form of the sectarian past. But it is not only this. The theme of distinctiveness is a means of countering the widespread trend in contemporary higher education toward mutual imitation among colleges and tasteless mass education. To the extent that it represents the former tendency today, it must be opposed. Insofar as it represents a counterisomorphic form, it needs to be channeled into more productive directions. Ironically, the quest for uniqueness has often been the occasion for intensification of imitative tendencies. For, after all, if a college believes it has discovered certain activities that insure its distinctiveness, even uniqueness, then it can safely let all other aspects of its curriculum and campus life be carbon copies of what occurs in similar colleges elsewhere.

Our central problem here is to examine the quest for uniqueness. If we can understand it with greater clarity, then we may at least be

---

[5] For example, see Wicke, op. cit., p. 2: "The insistent question is whether or not the church-related college has in fact a unique and essential role to play in American higher education."

warned against its perils and be in a better position to recognize and make use of its creative possibilities.

2. Response and Rejoinder

Varied answers have been given to the persistent question of how the church-related college can be unique. Some of these responses are outmoded and infrequently heard today. Others are superficial and unlikely to be entertained seriously by responsible educators and churchmen. Still further responses are probing and thoughtful and deserve consideration as goals toward which a college might strive.

In former times, still fresh in the memories of a few, the sectarian ethos governed the college and, in combination with characteristics of location and personal leadership, provided its distinctive goals and style. The sectarian sees himself as part of a small devoted group, surrounded by a godless multitude and called to live resolutely for his faith even in the face of persecution and temporary defeat. In a time when Christianity was a minority in American society, was seeking to restrain the excesses of the frontier, and was bringing a measure of faith and civilizing influence to the untamed West, the sectarian style, for all its narrow self-righteousness, probably played a creative role. As the frontier has disappeared and Christianity has become a majority movement, the problems of society and education have changed. Sectarianism, whatever evaluation is to be made of it in the nineteenth century, is now outmoded. Not imitation of past actions, but new responses are needed that stand in continuity with the commitment of the sectarian founders of Christian colleges and are relevant to the needs of contemporary constituencies. Quite clearly, what lent distinctiveness to these colleges in the past is not adequate now; much less can sectarianism be taken seriously today as a solution to the quest for uniqueness. Not many colleges today try to operate with a sectarian ethos, but a sizable number of church-related colleges have wealthy and influential persons in their constituencies who insure that pressure to retain elements from the sectarian past remains alive in the public present.

Some answers to the persistent question seem superficial and vague rather than outmoded. It has been said that the Christian college is unique because it provides education with a heart, a notion that makes more sense if one is confronting a kindly old professor than if one is dealt with by a flinthearted controller. Others say the Chris-

47

tian college is unique because it builds Christian character, makes good citizens, offers education with depth, develops faithful church members, etc. Answers of this kind are superficial in at least three ways: first, because the function affirmed is the result of too many factors to be credited alone to a college; second, because the goal is most often asserted uncritically, both as to general definition (i.e., what is Christian character?) and as to social meaning (i.e., does the college turn out staunch middle-class suburban types and call them Christian?); and third, because these affirmations are based on pious hopes and expected revenue for the college rather than on what actually does or does not occur there. More than superficial, many claims to uniqueness are dishonest gimmicks spawned for public-relations purposes and are related to operational realities in the most tenuous fashion.

Still other solutions to the quest for uniqueness are offered on a more substantial basis. Only a Christian college can provide Christian worship, offer instruction in religion, include challenge to and training in Christian living, discuss and communicate values, etc. Though all these functions can be phrased in ways that make them genuinely desirable in an educational setting, only those unacquainted with the actualities of private and public higher education and perhaps under the spell of charges that nonchurch schools are godless could believe that any of the functions named above is performed only at the church-related college and therefore makes it indispensable. State and private colleges can and do encompass all these operations within their campus communities, quite possibly in a more qualitative fashion than at many denominational institutions.

Lloyd J. Averill has suggested another answer to the question of uniqueness: "The Christian college has yielded one of the few things which gives it uniqueness, namely its *freedom to declare itself openly on the source of human good.*" [6] Apart from whether church-related colleges exhibit this characteristic generally, the issue remains as to whether such freedom can provide a uniqueness for the Christian college that inevitably sets it apart because this freedom is not possible in a private or public college. A vivid rejoinder to Averill's claim derives from my own memories as a student. At one school

---

[6] Lloyd J. Averill, A *Strategy for the Protestant College.* Philadelphia: Westminster Press, 1966, p. 60.

I attended, a state institution, I found Christian worship present and encouraged, opportunities for challenge to Christian faith and living powerfully present, and a magnificent president (along with many professors) who declared himself openly on the source of human good, took courageous action on behalf of Christian purposes, was a leader in his church, and supported students in their social concerns and actions. At a church-related institution with which I was later involved, these characteristics were scarcely present even in weakened form; at that time, there was also an amiable gentleman as president whose views even on trivial issues it was difficult to discover, much less on important social concerns and the source of human good. Though there exists no survey to provide careful information on the issue Averill raises, my own experiences in all parts of the nation make it clear that the persons in church, private, and public colleges have wide freedom, often unused, to declare themselves on the source of human good and to act to enhance that good among men. And my own observations lead me to suspect that as many persons with the courage to use that freedom will be found on public campuses as in either private or church-related colleges.

Even when put in the weaker and vaguer form favored by Pattillo and Mackenzie, the claim that the church-related college has unique resources sounds dubious. They write, "The principal assets of church institutions are: freedom to experiment and to serve special purposes, close student-faculty relationships, a creditable record of preparation for graduate and professional study, concern for the progress of individual students, and espousal of humane values." [7] In the one instance where it can be shown that church-related colleges perform better, i.e., larger proportion of students to professional schools, it is not clear that social background and financial ability are not more important than anything the college can or does in fact do. Pattillo and Mackenzie become even fainter in their praise: "A religious orientation should add a dimension to higher education that broadens and deepens the outlook of faculty and students alike, but we cannot say that this does in fact occur in most of the 817 institutions we have been studying." [8]

More important, however, the search for uniqueness in the opera-

[7] Pattillo and Mackenzie, op. cit., p. 100.
[8] Ibid., pp. 100-101.

tion of any Christian enterprise is dubious because it is basically defensive. It is an attempt to justify what is being done as though Christians have a monopoly on God's wisdom and sustaining power. I would agree with H. Richard Niebuhr that "self-defense is the most prevalent source of error in all thinking and perhaps especially in theology and ethics." [9]

This discussion raises two issues that deserve closer examination: first, whether or not operational uniqueness in the terms sought is possible, and second, whether, possible or not, it may be a dubiously Christian quest. I shall suggest that Christian faith leads in a quite different direction.

3. Is Operational Uniqueness Possible?

"Anything You Can Do, I Can Do Better" was a hit song on Broadway. It enjoys an even better run on the higher education circuit. The public and private colleges are singing it at the expense of the church institutions. Because they have more money, public colleges can usually do quite well whatever they set out to do. What public education does quantitatively, private education with no direct ties to the institutional church is probably doing qualitatively. All the activities Christian educators usually claim as unique for the church college are done and often done well at other institutions. I have become weary of the exclamatory sentence, "But we have courses in religion; no state school could have those!" uttered with total unawareness of the long-established departments of religion in certain state universities and the burgeoning of religious studies in public higher education across the nation.

Claims to uniqueness are made, I think, most often to project an image on behalf of good public relations. The uniqueness syndrome is misdirected. It is aimed at parents, church officials, and potential donors rather than at the more excellent operation of the college, that is, not at the formulation of education objectives that will serve as overall, long-range goals. It is also misconceived. None of the vaunted unique functions is necessarily Christian in itself. Anyone who has made the valiant attempt in a compulsory college chapel service to bring the students out of their customary news-

---

[9] H. Richard Niebuhr, *The Meaning of Revelation*. New York: Macmillan Co., 1941, p. viii.

paper-reading, studying, letter-writing, and dozing, is aware of a deep-seated problem. The answer to the question, "Isn't compulsory religion better than no religion?" has been given: "The difference between the two is imperceptible."

Actually, uniqueness as the discovery of a function for the church college that public and private institutions cannot perform is a will-o'-the-wisp, an ever receding goal. The isomorphic tendencies of higher education assure rapid imitation of one college by another when a program worthy of emulation appears. More perilous still, the illusory quest for uniqueness leads away from the central concerns of higher education and society, and therefore toward the periphery, toward increasing irrelevance.

A distinction must be made which we shall examine more closely later. Though I am convinced that there is probably no worthwhile educational function for the church-related college to perform by which it can be unique, which it is impossible for public and private institutions to do, this does not mean that various institutions— public, private, or church-related—may not choose to specialize in certain curricula, relate to particular social problems, and work with specific community groups and thus be operationally distinctive. By choosing purposes and roles related to its constituencies and to the needs of society around it, a college may be *distinguished from* other colleges and may even *become distinguished* in its performance. This means not that it does what other colleges *cannot* do but that it does what other colleges *are not* doing. It means finding its own vocation, discovering an identity for itself. This is both a Christian and an educationally fruitful direction in which to move.

4. Pride and Servanthood

The more we examine the quest of the church-related college for uniqueness, the more the suspicion is confirmed that such a quest arises from pride rather than from Christian faith. Wherever the pursuit of distinctive functions becomes a preoccupation, it is likely that public-relations motives have come to dominance over intentions to serve God and man. Claims that a particular institution performs functions no other college can equal are, with press releases of the administration, aimed principally at parents and church groups or at the maudlin memories of old grads.

Directed at parents, the claim to uniqueness is used most often to assure moms and dads that the college will perform effectively in protecting their offspring. The problem, of course, is that in our mobile American society no institution can do a very good job of protecting college-age youth from the time-honored temptations of late adolescence. College students know this and smirk at much of the administrative propaganda, and in their saner moments most parents are capable of recognizing the same thing. What the college may do, however, if its protectionist activities become dominant, is with deadening effectiveness to isolate the students from exciting educational opportunities. When the educational process is reduced to the dull confines satisfactory to fearful and guilt-ridden parents, then the studies that reveal how little reading is done by college graduates and how few take on community responsibilities become more comprehensible.

When claims to uniqueness are directed at church constituencies, the problems deriving from the sectarian past become more apparent. Courses in religion, it was once suggested, will make the students more religious, campus regulations will make them more moral, and compulsory chapel will assure their eternal commitment to the organized church. Such claims are often phrased to promote snob appeal, conveying in more or less subtle form the notion that Christian colleges somehow produce better people. Operationally this often means producing well-acculturated white Protestants (or devout and docile Catholics). Appeals to uniqueness are usually designed in part to reassure church groups that the student-products will faithfully support the denomination sponsoring the college.

It is small wonder that students in increasing numbers have become rebels against required religion courses, compulsory chapel attendance, and restrictive campus regulations. They recognize that these parts of the college operation are aimed over their heads at parents and church bodies rather than being intended to serve recognized educational purposes.

There is much talk today of the church as servant. It is talked about more than it is practiced, and nowhere is this disjunction more apparent than among the church-related colleges. One way to view the problem is in terms of the gap between the projected image of the college and the reality of its operation. Quite clearly there is a mounting credibility gap from the standpoint of the students, and the better the student, the wider the gap is likely to be—so yawning, in fact, that he is likely to transfer elsewhere or drop out.

The divergence between the image and reality aside, however, there may be a more important problem: does not the reality need rethinking? It seems to occur infrequently to church officials and institutions that actions arising from genuine attempts at servanthood might prove to be better public relations than ill-concealed efforts at institutional self-serving. This problem poses one of the central dilemmas of the churches today, one felt with special keenness by both college students and sensitive adults. Some studies suggest that the present college generation is open to religious faith but is "turned off" by the organizational aggrandizement they regard as characteristic of institutional Christianity. One suspects that similar reactions may be present among the most thoughtful and concerned of the "over thirties" as well. In a movement centered upon a crucified Lord, societal success may prove to be catastrophic failure. Certainly some of the best publicity the churches have received over the past decade has come when building programs were put aside and dangers to the budget forgotten, and venturesome attempts to serve the cause of civil rights and human betterment were undertaken. It is possible that the same thing would prove true of the church-related college.

To speak of pride and servanthood places the dilemma of the church-related college in new and illuminating perspective. We have been speaking of the problem of sectarian past versus public present. Now we contrast protectionist pride with open servanthood. To pose the dilemma in this way suggests that the quest for uniqueness more than being an impossible pursuit, may actually subvert the deeper Christian purposes of the church-related college. The more a college strives toward an ephemeral distinctiveness, the more it may be tempted to deny the claims of Christian faith upon it, claims that demand involved servanthood and active witness for social justice.

The colonial colleges, the ones I have called public Christian colleges, were closely related both to the Christian heritage and to the needs of the society around them as these were perceived. These colleges were founded to perform functions on behalf of the entire community. They sought to serve the good of the whole. In the case of each of these colleges, as it was the only one around, it was scarcely troubled by the quest for uniqueness. From our twentieth-century viewpoint we may regard as somewhat narrow the purposes these colleges were founded to serve, but in their own time the scope of their aims was intended to include the colony of which each was a part and not merely a sector of it.

To serve the inclusive purposes of a whole community critically and Christianly interpreted is a more appropriate source of operational criteria for a church-related college than isolated distinctiveness and uniqueness. Whatever genuinely serves the needs and aspirations of a diverse community may be done by public or private colleges as well or better than by the church-related. Joining with the Christian movement at its better moments in all ages, the church-related college may pioneer in advancing the common good, in serving the downtrodden and oppressed, and in opening new possibilities for a more humane society. And informed by Christian faith, the church-related college should rejoice when other colleges or community groups join in advancing these efforts; surely this is more consonant with our Christian heritage in its aspirations and actions to serve the cause of humanity than seeking separation in a dubious uniqueness. The search for uniqueness is the most pervasive and persistent form the remnants of the sectarian past take in the public present, and it may also be the greatest roadblock in seeking to resolve the identity crisis and becoming a responsible college.

Chapter IV

CHRISTIAN FAITH
AND HIGHER EDUCATION

WE HAVE SUGGESTED that the quest for uniqueness of function tempts church-related colleges into prideful claims that undermine rather than fulfill Christian faith. The same temptation undoubtedly exists and is often yielded to by other sectors of the Christian movement—by residential parishes, by "experimental" ministries, by denominational officials, and most clearly by theologians who place a unique function of theology or pursuit of their own professional status and reputation above the cause of God.

Admitting this temptation, what understanding of response and responsibility more faithful to the Christian heritage than uniqueness is available for shaping the purposes and functions of colleges and other activities seeking to be informed by Christian faith? The answer to this must be sought and formulated theologically. But it must be theological in a way that gives guidance for the decisions and actions of human living rather than being only an exercise in historical exploration or systematic construction of doctrine.

In *Church-Sponsored Higher Education in the United States,* Pattillo and Mackenzie correctly point out that church-sponsored colleges and universities have serious theological problems, and they trace these problems especially to the confusion in theology resulting from "the secularization of life and thought in recent centuries." They quote James M. Gustafson: "The dilemma is that the church represents 'a historical tradition which in many respects is dissonant with contemporary knowledge and with the principles of practical life in the age of technology'" so that "'in the secularization of modern life God is very remote to most men.'"[1]

This is an unhappy and probably inaccurate way to state the theological problems of our time. Gustafson's words suggest it is the historical tradition of Christian faith that is at odds with the contemporary world. This may be correct in much the same sense as the formulations of Newton and Lavoisier may be said to be at dissonance with present-day physics and chemistry. But to draw from this that the scientific tradition is at odds with contemporary knowledge and experience would scarcely be adequate. Any physicist today who repeated the notions of Newton uncritically would be violating the scientific tradition, not representing it. In parallel fashion, the fault appears to be that theologians are trapped within the past—to defend its formulations rigidly in some instances, to repeat past formulations with minor variations, or to react uncritically against it. All too seldom do we find theologians taking up the hard task of wrestling with theological issues as they arise in present form.

It is not that Christian faith is necessarily dissonant with life in a technological age or that God is remote from man but rather that neither churches nor theologians have done an adequate job of showing the ways in which the characteristics of our time referred to very loosely as "secularization" illumine and are illumined by the historical faith of Bible and Christian heritage. Frederick Sontag may be correct in this appraisal of the contemporary theological scene:

> The main impression is that we are in *a lull after the storm*. Bonhoeffer is gone. Tillich, Barth, Bultmann, and Niebuhr were all born well before the turn of the century and had the peak of their influence a generation ago. One cannot say that their views are now disturbing the scene or upsetting old patterns. . . . After such a generation of giants and of revolutions in direction, an extended calm is almost to be expected.[2]

We can ill afford a lull in theological effort today when society is developing and changing with an accelerating pace. The problems multiply and insight from many directions is needed. Not least

---

[1] Pattillo and Mackenzie, op. cit., p. 135, quoting from Gustafson, "The Clergy in the United States," *Daedalus*, vol. 92, no. 4 (Fall, 1963).

[2] Frederick Sontag, *The Future of Theology*. Philadelphia: Westminster Press, 1969, p. 43.

among our needs is reflective wrestling with encompassing issues as they present themselves today; this is and always has been the central task of theology.

In this chapter we shall make a tentative beginning at the theological task that must be done. To the extent that the effort is significant, the relation of Christian faith to present social realities and to the ultimate issues pressing in upon us in those realities will be indicated in ways that illumine the purposes and functions of church-related higher education, that is, aid in resolving the institutional crisis of identity.

1. Toward an Incarnational Theology

Because of the diversity of Christian believing and living, there are many possible points of beginning in seeking to make clear the living wholeness of Christian faith in its close relation with humanity, its world, and its problems. For many reasons, we shall begin as Christians with Jesus Christ.

The historical center of Christian faith is Jesus Christ. From the standpoint of the emergence of the Christian movement, Jesus Christ as the point of faith's beginning is clear. The first confession of faith, "Jesus is Lord," indicates the controlling position faith in him assumed in the growth of doctrine and creeds. But Jesus Christ points beyond himself to his Father, to God the Creator, and to God the Holy Spirit, that imminent force in church and humanity, in all societies and all histories. To begin with Jesus Christ in the experience of faith is to find ourselves confronted by the triune God and to enter upon the way of response to God's redemptive power in all events.

It is no less important to begin with Jesus Christ in seeking policy for church colleges than in dealing with parish worship or church school curriculum. The specific context of higher education and societal relations will require different terms and direction of discussion, but focus upon the faithful, renewing force set loose upon human history in Cross and Resurrection must be present in all.

To begin with God the creator has a deceptive attractiveness, going back to the first words of Genesis: "In the beginning God. . . ." Unless we remember that the meaning of these words is not self-evident but is given content by the Hebrew-Christian history of

57

Exodus, prophecy, and, above all for Christians, Jesus Christ, giving priority to the action of God leads inevitably toward radical skepticism, a recent form of which is the "God is dead" movement. In similar fashion, according centrality to some ontological principle usually ends in various rationalistic idolatries, and focus upon social phenomena may drift into pluralistic relativism for lack of historical realism.

To begin with Jesus Christ means also to begin with the Incarnate Lord. In the view of Christian faith, he is fully God and fully man, a way of stating the matter that has difficulties mathematically and in terms of classical metaphysics but is eminently satisfactory on historical grounds. The completely human Jesus is believed in as anointed with divine function in historical experience. As Incarnate, he is the enfleshment of the most sovereign reality of human experiencing and historical awareness.

Though the incarnational view in its best-known form is found in the prologue to the Gospel of John, Philippians presents this perspective in an especially interesting way:

> Let each of you look not only to his own interests, but also to the interests of others. Have this mind among yourselves, which you have in Christ Jesus, who, though he was in the form of God, did not count equality with God a thing to be grasped, but emptied himself, taking the form of a servant, being born in the likeness of men. And being found in human form he humbled himself and became obedient unto death, even death on a cross. Therefore God has highly exalted him and bestowed on him the name which is above every name, that at the name of Jesus every knee should bow, in heaven and on earth and under the earth, and every tongue confess that Jesus Christ is Lord, to the glory of God the Father (Philippians 2:4-11).

Here is the "secular" Jesus Christ, to apply the popular catchword of the present moment. Emptied of all transcendence, in thoroughly human form, he humbles himself. And through the self-emptying, the humbling, and the very human death, he is exalted as Lord. By giving up all claim to anything that would set him apart from human existence and experience, by becoming Incarnate, Jesus Christ takes up his function as Lord and Saviour. Rather than by way of uniqueness, otherness, or transcendence, the way of Jesus Christ's lordship is that of total solidarity with humanity. Christians in their seeking to follow him are called away from efforts at uniqueness to actions affirming solidarity.

In one of his most luminous passages Karl Barth suggests much the same thing. In his section on reconciliation, he discusses the Christian community as it exists in mission within the world. Rather than following the usual treatment today, which views church and world as separate, opposing entities, he holds that the Christian community knows itself through Jesus Christ to be in solidarity with the world and responsible for it.[3] Surely this view is more consonant with faith in the Incarnate Lord of Philippians than the pride that leads to the affirmation of a chasm between church and world. Christian faith requires us, whatever the arena of our lives, to confess our solidarity in sin, in limited capabilities, and in our stunted love, with the world in which we find ourselves, and to act in awareness of our responsibility for it. This insight can be as instructive for church-related colleges as for Christians elsewhere. The call of the Incarnate One to us is not that we forget Christian faith and become secular but that in Christian faith we live in solidarity with our fellow human beings and our society.

2. Christ and Creation

To speak of solidarity with our world relates us at once to creation and to an ethic focused upon Jesus Christ. In ethics, failure to begin with Jesus Christ requires a quest for alternative foundations for moral action such as natural law or secularity. Resort to ontological or natural or secular criteria in theology and ethics is regarded as necessary because traditional formulations do not do justice to the importance of the created order or do not provide adequate involvement with the world. The effect of these approaches is to place Jesus Christ in a secondary position and to interpret him in light of the analysis of some other reality. Though the "death of God" and the "secular" theologians retain a touching piety in regard to Jesus, he is not central to their theological-ethical method. One reason for these unhappy solutions is the excessive emphasis in the Western tradition of theology upon the soteriological significance of Jesus Christ and inadequate attention to the creational meaning of Christ. Jesus is seen as saviour, performing a redemptive function, but he is not

---

[3] Karl Barth, *Church Dogmatics*, IV/3/2. Edinburgh, 1962, pp. 762-795.

seen as Lord of creation. This problem derives from the correlation of Christ with human sin, so that the incarnation is seen "as contingent upon the occurrence of sin." [4] Jesus Christ is Redeemer, but the creational significance of Incarnation is in no way dependent upon sin.

Jesus Christ as Lord of creation is prior to Jesus Christ as Redeemer, and the latter meaning must be affirmed as a function of the former. Redemption is not needed merely because of man's fall, because of sin. Jesus Christ as Redeemer is the Incarnate Lord who continues and fulfills the process initiated in creation; the Incarnate One performs a task set in God's creative intention, a task achieved in the light of sin but not a function that would have been unnecessary without sin. For Christian faith and action, Incarnation directs our attention to the triune God, to creation in process toward a goal as well as to the Logos become flesh. [5]

Jesus Christ as the Logos of God becoming flesh, as the Incarnate Lord, may well be that central conviction of Christian faith by which we can understand most clearly the importance of higher education and the purposes and roles of colleges under church sponsorship. Certainly, Incarnation can remind us that the basis of Christian decision and action in higher education as elsewhere is the creating, governing, redeeming action of God within events themselves rather than the individual or collective presence of Christians seeking unique functions in an entity vaguely designated as "the secular world."

Incarnation calls us back to our beginning point in the presence of Jesus Christ as the basis of the entire created order, of society and human relationship, of the sovereign power in human experience, and of the possibility of intelligible exploration and learning. This is the clearest meaning of the prologue to the Gospel of John: "In the beginning was the [Logos], and the [Logos] was with God, and the [Logos] was God. He was in the beginning with God; all things were made through him, and without him was not anything made that was made" (John 1:1-3). Hebrews opens with a similar assertion:

---

[4] See Herbert W. Richardson, *Toward an American Theology*. New York: Harper & Row, 1967, pp. 127-28.

[5] Cf. St. Athanasius, *On the Incarnation*. London, 1953: "The renewal of creation has been wrought by the Self-same Word Who made it in the beginning. There is thus no inconsistency between creation and salvation" (p. 26).

". . . but in these last days he has spoken to us by a Son, whom he appointed the heir of all things, through whom also he created the world. He reflects the glory of God and bears the very stamp of his nature, upholding the universe by his word of power" (Hebrews 1:2-3a). The sovereign power of creation, in virtue of which there are order, relation, and intelligibility, has become enfleshed in Jesus Christ. Incarnation is the charter of the intellectual enterprise, when it is seen in Christian perspective. The Incarnate Lord is the starting point for a theological understanding of higher education that can provide a basis for decision and action.

Our problem is never to bolster the power and vitality of an ineffectual, dying deity. Instead, it is finding ways to respond to the awesome power of God coursing through natural and historical occurrence. This power which surrounds us bears us and our companions along on a rushing, tumultuous stream of events. Our problem is that this reality from which there is in life no escape seems filled with threat to all we prize. Despair and death seem the end of all our striving. It is not God as dead but God the alive destroyer who confronts us. It is human hope that may well perish. In this situation, Jesus Christ as the Logos of reality become Incarnate can give hope and courage to confront an apparently threatening reality, insight for response, and strength to move into an uncertain future. These results are effected not by handing man a complete blueprint of reality but by calling forth in the life, death, and resurrection of the Incarnate One trust in the onrushing power of events.

Incarnation, when understood creationally as well as redemptively, requires response as an action challenging us within the realities of the created order, in all occasions of relation and meaning, and in situations of decision and action. A creational Jesus Christ is a "secular" Jesus Christ in the faddist jargon, but he is making all things "sacred" in his renewing power. In him Christians discover their solidarity with all that is natural, biological, and human and their responsibility within the order and disorder of experienced events. Such a view does not seek to eliminate doctrine and worship in an effort to achieve a "religionless Christianity." Rather it sees the church as "an arrow within the world directed toward the future" (Jürgen Moltmann), as a movement in "permanent revolution" (H. Richard Niebuhr), constantly transforming and being transformed by the power at work within and around it. The church as the continuing witness to the Incarnate Lord is seen not only in the past history of the churches but also in the sovereign love present in the Logos of world occurrence as disclosed in Jesus Christ.

This view discloses the inadequate rendering of Logos into English as Word, meaning to most persons today a sound of the voice or letters on a page. The author of John used Greek, but he sought to convey the force of the Hebrew *dabar*, the meaning of which in English would be better rendered as *covenant action* than sound of a voice. The sentence, "I give you my word," conveys the only English usage of Word with a meaning approaching *dabar*. Incarnation is not a word but the covenant action of God from creation to consummation made flesh. This is the glory Christians discover in the human Jesus, in virtue of which they believe in him as Christ.

In a similar way the usual distinction between church and world, virtually a cliché in much contemporary theology, endangers our understanding of Christian ministry through its tendency to regard Jesus Christ as ecclesiastical property and his presence in the world as dependent upon the words and actions of those who have responded in faith to the preached Word. The action challenging us in Scripture, in sacrament, in preaching, conveys both creation and redemption in Jesus Christ. In worship and study of the Bible, in situations of human relation and hurt, Christians discover themselves called by the Lord of nature and history, whose power is manifest in nuclear fusion and the fall of empires. In God's address to them within the pain and possibility of real events, Christians become aware that nature is not law but grace, that the gospel is not an addendum to creation but its ground and purpose, that God's action toward man and his response is within the decisions and work of society and social responsibility, not apart from them.

Christians do not transport Jesus Christ from church premises to the world. Rather he is there through creation, long preceding them, calling them to responsible participation in that sector of the world called higher education, through the actions of university administration, teaching, research, and study; through the decisions of policy in which college, society, and church are related to and shape human life. In faith we discover Jesus Christ confronting us in the tangled personal relations of a residence hall, in the hard grind of producing a paper, in the care required to experiment, in the action of the college in bettering its community, in the anxiety of decisions, and in the pain of facing the realities of our lives in family and society. He judges the impersonality of mass education, the frayed integrity of academic research, and the superficial community of academic discipline and college dormitory. He is present as Redeemer in the shared community of achievement, in the persistent goal of a more humane world, and in the development of human tools of reconciliation.

Incarnation suggests that most important for Christians is not *their* presence but rather the presence of Jesus Christ. Christian "presence" does not mean primarily that a group of believers has at last arrived on the scene and is making its witness and influence felt. Without belittling the importance of Christian responsibility for the relationships and meaning within which Christians find themselves, the secondary, "responsive" character of their presence must be emphasized. Christians could not respond to God if he did not first call them to his service. Nor could witness and influence bear fruit unless they are used of God. A college as an enterprise of Christians makes sense only because of the prior presence of Jesus Christ, and we need the constant reminder that this is the case.

Even further, however, Incarnation reminds us that God's work of judgment and reconciliation takes place without and apart from the presence of Christians. By the covenant action in creation, as seen in Christian faith, the presence of God is within the learning and relations of the university whether a community of believers is at work or not. When H. Richard Niebuhr spoke once of "the grace of doing nothing," he was not recommending inaction as a general principle. Instead he was pointing to God as "the structure in things, the source of all meaning, the 'I am that I am,' that which is that it is. He is the rock against which we beat in vain, that which bruises and overwhelms us when we seek to impose our wishes, contrary to his, upon him." He is the "structure of the universe," the "creative will" of all creation.[6] For Christian faith, this reality of God as manifest in creation is the primary presence in every occasion.

But this reality toward which the Incarnation directs our attention has crucial importance for the response of Christians within the tasks set for them by their locations as student, professor, or administrator.

---

[6] H. Richard Niebuhr, "A Communication," *The Christian Century*, April 6, 1932, p. 447.

We are confronted and called by God in Jesus Christ not on the periphery of life but at its center. Christian responsibility makes demands at the core of human need and action rather than at the unimportant edge of our communities. Christians are called to the center of campus purposes and decisions. Gathering for worship and reflection in faith does not fulfill itself if its goal becomes the initiation and perpetuation of a Christian "ghetto" where frosting of dubious flavor is put on the cake of youth's college experience. The call of the crucified and risen Lord demands our participation to the full limit of our abilities and our insight, and reveals to us our solidarity with the human community.

Incarnation involves us in recognizing the central significance of the enterprise of learning not only for the university and society but also for Christian faith. Christian response within a campus does not consist only of a one-way flow of interpretation from the Christian tradition to academicians. It means also openness, receiving, learning, as occasions provide new and wider understanding of Christian faith.

Initially the significance of learning for Christian faith rests upon the origins of the world at the hands of God. The entire universe, in Christian perspective, is sacred by its creation through Jesus Christ. It is therefore worthy of the devout and rigorous attention of Christians. The conservation and enhancement of the world as we find it rather than its abuse and destruction is an obvious corollary of Christian convictions about creation. The implications for learning are no less clear, though they have often been ignored and violated by Christians seeking to defend their limited conceptions of God and his works. The activity of scholarship is as necessary to Christian faith as is breathing to the human body. Learning means also inviting and welcoming the risks inherent in the enterprise. Views of the cosmos held by churchmen in the past have been overturned, to the profit of man and faith. Cherished beliefs have been called into question, usually forcing Christian thinkers to discard spurious or irrelevant meanings. Painful as this process may be, it is essential if Christianity is not to settle into a mire of antiquated notions and replace faith in the living God with idolatrous loyalty to an ever dying past.

The impetus of Christian faith toward learning means that Christians are called in scholarship to investigate rigorously the entire created order. On the one hand, there is knowledge that can aid in making the world more human. On the other hand, nature and history as spheres of scholarly endeavor provide a widening knowledge of the covenant action through which the world is made. Certainly nature and history partly disclose and partly conceal their Creator. There is no clear or simple movement from learning to faith. But the act (Logos) made flesh reveals the act (Logos) made world, and the universe as it is discovered and rediscovered in the painstaking analyses of the academic community continues to inform faith in Jesus Christ as it seeks understanding and constantly discloses to faith new possibilities for the meaning of God that extend beyond our limited conceptions.

When man's faith rests in God rather than seeking an illusory security in old doctrinal formulae, then it becomes possible to affirm that all intellectual endeavor, whether by those calling themselves Christian or not, is response to the same creation and to the Creator. Freud's anti-Christian convictions are clear. Many have thought, therefore, that he had nothing to offer the Christian community. Through the medium of those who took the work of his genius seriously, Freud has aided in the recovery of an understanding of man with Pauline, Augustinian, and Lutheran depth and has opened new and exciting ways of pastoral care.

In the same fashion, the knowledge and skills of higher education can be utilized to solve human problems and shape an environment better suited for human habitation. When work needs to be done to prevent further pollution of nature and overcome urban blight and racial injustice, one does not examine the faith-commitments of those who are doing research but rather whether or not their work is useful. The cause of man—and the ecumenical movement—has been advanced when persons and communities joined in addressing human need without first dividing themselves according to doctrinal convictions. Christians are called in the Christ of creation to appropriate knowledge from any source and to enter whatever alliances will further the cause of love and peace.

Incarnation serves also as a constant reminder, to Christians as to others, that, whatever varieties of meanings man may assign to truth, we cannot rest in a view confined solely to propositions and functions but must also take account of the purpose and relation we strive to express in the word love. Jesus Christ stands as judgment upon our narrow, impersonal conceptions of truth and for a wider view that encompasses the uses to which knowledge is put within the goals of man.

This perspective must not, however, be regarded as a plea for a unified world view in the university. Just the opposite is intended. The diversity of academic viewpoints is opened to us through Christian faith, and the necessity of taking the variety seriously is affirmed. Not only do we learn to be grateful for the companions who confront us with the limits of our vision, but we see also that the academic context of rigor and disagreement may become an arena of God's self-revelation and call to commitment as surely as a candle-lit sanctuary or a private session of agonized self-recrimination and repentance.

This incarnational perspective makes possible a view of a church-related college as called in Christian faith to abandon pretensions to uniqueness and to address the tasks set by human needs and aspirations. A new identity, one consistent with both Christian faith and social responsibility, can be discovered through affirming solidarity with creation, society, and the human condition.

3. Solidarity and Responsibility

When self-awareness in Christian faith leads to an understanding of solidarity with the creation and with the whole human community, then responsibility takes on renewed meaning. Furthermore, it is in elaborating the significance of responsibility in Christian faith that the task of the church-related college can be clarified within the theological perimeter already provided. We have suggested that a new identity for the church-related college emerges from an understanding of itself in solidarity with its constituencies, with its society, and with the created, human order. To seek for uniqueness is not only operationally impossible but also leads to a separatist style of dubious Christian validity. This solidarity derives from an incarnational faith in Jesus Christ encompassing creation through him as well as the historical community centered in him.

Responsibility, when understood incarnationally, involves (1) the character and context of response, (2) the criteria of action, and (3) the style of the faithful deed. Though subsequent chapters will add concreteness to the meaning of responsibility for a church-related college, we can provide the connective tissue that relates incarnational faith to particular experiences and alternatives and enables one to see specific situations as opportunities for responsible decision and action.

Most obviously, responsibility means the *ability to respond,* the power to act. But implied also is a context of interaction, in which every act is in response to prior actions and in expectation of further action. It is not an action in and of itself, if one can even consider it in isolation, that gives it moral significance but rather the way in which it forms part of a series of actions and responses, that is, in terms of the antecedent actions to which it is response,[7] the resultant series emerging from it, and the entire pattern of which it is part. H. Richard Niebuhr, one of the major figures of theology and ethics in this century, has put this element of responsibility as follows: "For the ethics of responsibility, the *fitting* action, the one that fits into a total interaction as response and as anticipation of further response, is alone conducive to the good and alone is right." [8]

But response must not be confused with involuntary reaction. Responsibility implies also an *awareness* of the interaction *and reflection* upon how actions fit into the series. Actions that are accompanied by no reflection on their role in a chain of responses could scarcely be regarded as responsible. On the one hand, this reflection concerns the meaning of the process of interaction as past, future, and pattern-connecting events and actions. How are the actions to which one responds to be understood? On the other hand, moral reflection concerns the shaping of the response to be made, how this action is to be fitted into a process already under way so as to produce results and new interaction regarded as good. What we regard as responsible action requires reflection on what is going on in our society and our world and what action will relate this process to goals we wish to achieve, that is, involvement with social policy.

Responsibility also means *participation in this ongoing interaction* into which actions fit or do not fit, tend to produce desired results and good ends, or fail. Accountability to others and for the future makes responsible agents. To take a single action for racial justice

---

[7] See Thomas C. Oden, *Radical Obedience.* Philadelphia: Westminster Press, 1964, pp. 9-10, for a brief discussion of the ways in which "obedience" in English no longer conveys the element of response contained in the Hebrew, Greek, and German equivalents. This may explain in part the fairly recent rise of the term "responsibility" to prominence in ethical discussion.

[8] H. Richard Niebuhr, *The Responsible Self.* New York: Harper & Row, 1963, p. 61. This section owes much to Niebuhr's treatment of responsibility.

and fail to follow up with further actions or grapple with the consequences of the prior deed could not be called responsible. It is this continuing participation that makes reflective response an issue in responsible action.

The combination of these elements—response, reflection, continuing participation—means that responsibility must be understood as *solidarity* with the vitalities, persons, and configurations of social interaction. No one of these elements has importance apart from an ongoing community of agents, apart from an awareness of the indissoluble relation among human actions. "The idea or pattern of responsibility," Niebuhr writes, "may summarily and abstractly be defined as the idea of an agent's action as response to an action upon him in accordance with his interpretation of the latter action and with his expectation of response to his response; and all of this is in a continuing community of agents." [9]

In speaking of responsibility as we have, one must not assume that responsibility applies only to individual persons and not to colleges, governments, or other groups. Social solidarity implies that "individuals" cannot be understood "individualistically" but come to self-awareness and perform as agents within communal interrelations. In similar manner, social groups with even minimal cohesiveness have a "selfhood" defined in terms of the systems of relations within which they exist. Responsibility inheres in centers of response, reflection, and continuing participation, within a process defined by social solidarity.

Christian responsibility understood incarnationally involves criteria of action. Viewed in one way, criteria are the reflective, evaluative dimension of responsibility. From another perspective, they are the valent powers shaping action. If one rejects the dualism of mind and body, then valuing and valency are distinguishable but inseparable elements in all human action.

In similar fashion, the historical Jesus Christ and the creational Jesus Christ are not seen in dualistic form as a Jesus of history over against a Christ of faith or as institutionalized tradition versus a changing present. Instead, the historical and creational are distinguishable but inseparable elements comprising faith in the Incarnation of Jesus Christ. The historical which is interpenetrated by

---

[9] Ibid., p. 65.

creation is constantly renewed, expanded, and protected from being reduced to the past. Creation as new occurrence forces the reshaping of historical vision and thus keeps the future and the "new" as elements of history.[10] Historical understanding, on the other hand, provides the firm but tentative ordering of faith adequate for human action within the diversity of the moving creation and alternative communities of interpretation.

To speak of the incarnational Jesus Christ is not to abandon criteria for action but rather to insist that present and future as well as past must enter into the shaping of action. Purposes, norms, and present realities are interrelated in formulating criteria for decisions.

First, policies, decisions, and actions are informed by goals perceived as desirable. For Christians, these goals derive from the biblical sense of promise and hope that are given content by the human potentialities revealed in Israel and in Jesus Christ. Justice and love among men shape action toward the future. Specific social wrongs are made targets for elimination. Programs to meet certain needs of particular human groups are developed. But promise and hope give a contingent character to all plans, and the anticipation of obsolescence governs all program development. Goals and programs come into being through reflective faith in Jesus Christ but are regarded as providing the basis of present decisions and actions, not as unchanging ultimates.

Second, criteria of action derive from norms and actions remembered from the near and distant past. The Mosaic commandments, the parables of Jesus, the social achievements of Christian churches, the affirmations of the Declaration of Independence and the Constitution, the political programs of Jackson, Lincoln, and Roosevelt— all these provide specific rules and illustrations by which present criteria are shaped. The present repeats and imitates the past. But a sense of an opening future prevents that repetition and imitation from becoming a petrified betrayal of the hope contained in the past. In saying, "You have heard that it was said. . . . But I say to you," and "Think not that I have come to abolish the law and the prophets . . . but to fulfill them" (cf. Matthew 5:17-48), Jesus illus-

---

[10] For a brilliant treatment of this theme of the "new," see Ernst Bloch, *Das Prinzip Hoffnung*, Frankfurt am Main: Suhrkamp, 1959.

trates and provides authority for appropriating the past by changing and lifting it toward the hope it embodies.

Third, Christian responsibility requires that actions be based upon wide and careful understanding of present relations and needs. Just as action in the immediate situation neither makes sense nor is responsible if it ignores the larger context of reality present in meaning and hope, so decisions uninformed about the present context will be neither appropriate nor responsible. To give a freezing but well-fed man a year's supply of food can find its equally absurd parallels in employment training for jobs that have been phased out and liberal arts programs unconcerned with making the world and its inhabitants more human. Responsible action today requires investigation and complex data. But inquiry is conducted and the use of information made within the perspectives provided by prophetic critique and Christian hope.

Fourth, what has already been suggested, vision of future possibility, the examples and guidance from the past, and careful understanding of the present situation must be brought together into action that fits faithfully into the interaction among men and between human society and the reality of divine governance. Reflective, informed wisdom must be integrated into decisive, well-administered action. This balancing of elements to shape specific programs and decisions may be called the covenantal or federal criterion of action.

This understanding of responsibility and criteria gives shape to the faithful deed. Combining perspectives from past, present, and future gives comprehensiveness to the faithful deed. Infusion of the biblical sense of promise and hope lends historical fittingness to the faithful deed. Anticipation of the new provides flexibility and change in the faithful deed. And careful attention to data about present realities adds precision to the faithful deed.

4. Identity and the Common Good

A new identity for the church-related college will emerge from a view of its solidarity within society rather than through defining its separateness. In the perspective of Christian faith this sense of solidarity derives from an incarnational understanding of Jesus Christ and implies responsibility with and for the present and potential constituencies of the college. It is, however, necessary to say more carefully what these constituencies are, what solidarity means, and how responsibility in these terms points toward solutions to the identity crisis.

The most obvious constituencies of any college are those visible in the immediate present. One thinks immediately of trustees as the body vested with legal ownership and control and of the president and his administrative personnel who exercise governance on behalf of trustees. The president remains in office only as long as the trustees have confidence in his leadership. Without belaboring the point or dealing with the complexities of these relationships, we may say that the task of retaining the confidence of the trustees in the president only appears simpler if the president and his staff provide the primary information about and interpretation of college purposes, program, and support. Alternative sources of data about higher education in general as well as this college in particular—from the mass media, from accrediting agencies and other external evaluations, federal and foundation studies, etc.—make possible more rigorous criteria of the president's performance and the greater likelihood that "credibility gaps" will develop. But the increasing independence of faculty because of professional organizations and mobility over the past few decades and the emergence of student power in the sixties compound the problem and have been bringing on acute cases of "presidential fatigue" among college administrators. Any book about presidents and trustees written before the Berkeley Free Speech Movement of 1964 is almost certain to be out of date today. Students once could be safely regarded as a "client" constituency, but no longer is this possible. Students are demanding and acquiring a voice in campus governance and must therefore be regarded as a participating constituency in higher education. As competent faculty members came into short supply in the academic marketplace after World War II, they acquired increased power, in part directly in regard to internal policy matters and in part indirectly through the veto power provided them in opportunities to move to other institutions. Dealing with the competing demands of these immediate constituencies presents a situation fraught with mounting difficulties for college presidents. Constituencies that provide funds must also be cultivated and enlarged: church bodies, wealthy donors, industry and businesses, foundations, and parents. The community served by the college, local, regional, and in some cases national, must also be considered. These are the major groups of the immediate present

71

that must be taken into account in setting the goals and operational style of a college.

The only constituencies, however, to be considered are not those of the immediate present. To take them alone into account can easily lead to short-range goals and even opportunism. There are also constituencies of the past to be considered. The founders of the college and leaders in its life since then who sought a responsible role for the college in their own time; the community of higher education stretching back through colonial America to the medieval schools and Greek academies; the striving to be faithful to God through learning and through tasks of society which have informed that "great cloud of witnesses" in the midst of which we perform all our labors.

And there are also constituencies of the future that must be kept in mind. To develop the roles and functions appropriate for college today one must have some conception of the direction in which it and society will move. Given its past and present constituencies, realistic appraisals must be made of future possibilities as to what student constituencies, what financial resources, what new relationships with industry, government, and community institutions, would be in keeping with the life of the college and its resources.

A new identity for the college will emerge when these constituencies of the past, present, and future are brought into the planning that shapes the workings of this collegiate community. Recognizing the life of the college as involved with these constituencies, with their needs and purposes, with their common good and functioning, is the meaning of solidarity, and to develop the college in the light of this solidarity is the meaning of responsibility to God for a particular academic community.

Just as responsibility to God must be specified, so also is it necessary to examine the meaning of "common good." There is probably no such thing as a simple common good for any human community, given the fantastic diversity present everywhere in the world today. In the first place, to speak of the common good can be much too abstract. And in the second place, the differences of needs and purposes of various persons and groups make it impossible to evolve a single good for the whole. Nevertheless, the Prophet Jeremiah was not speaking idly but rather seeking to enunciate the will of God for Israel when he wrote to the exiles in Babylon, "But seek the welfare of the city where I have sent you into exile, and pray to the Lord on its behalf, for in its welfare you will find your welfare" (Jeremiah 29: 7).

The common good must be thought of neither as some abstract principle such as justice or love, nor can it be considered apart from the diverse components and competing needs and interests present in every human community. The common good must be understood through that which is good for all, and this can never be reduced in particular situations to a single good.

Human communities are made up of individuals and groups whose interests may sometimes be parallel but more often run at varying angles to one another and quite often are in direct conflict. Maintaining these diverse interests under general conditions of order without completely suppressing the interests of any is the difficult task of a democratic society. Limited disorder must be permitted in order that those who believe some interests are being suppressed may protest. And it is inevitable that some interests at odds with the overwhelming views of the society will be denied. The political process of a democracy is that of providing channels for the interests of diverse factions through political parties and elections, to be partly accommodated so that all major interests are included and no substantial minor groupings excluded. Democracy is thus not a means for defining an abstract common good but rather a political system for working out inclusive compromises among the interests and perceived goods of a diverse population.

One prominent stream of Christian faith has provided an important force in the development of democracy. This is the federal or covenantal theology most prominent in the Reformed churches of Switzerland, the German Rhineland, the Netherlands, Britain, and New England. The federal perspective sees man in solidarity and responsibility before God in virtue of his creation at the hands of the covenant God. Human community is shaped by man's response, proximately in terms of his own interest and perceived good and ultimately by the reality of nature and history under the sovereignty of the One who is eternally faithful. Democracy fits in well with this federal theology and provides probably the best political process so far developed by man for including the widest spectrum of interests within a given society. The democratic process, however, has often overlooked an element present in its federal background, an element recognized keenly by such constitutional fathers as James Madison and his mentors among the colonial federalists. This element is that man's perceived interests are not always his real interests, that the goods he strives for are not always the goods he really wants, and the conviction that a more inclusive force is at work in part overruling the interests of each of us. Abraham Lincoln expressed this view most directly in his second Inaugural Address on March 4, 1865, when he said of the competing interests that brought on the Civil War: "Both read the same Bible and pray to the same God. . . . The prayers of both could not be answered. That of neither has been answered fully. The Almighty has His own purposes."

Christians acting within a democratic order respond with a sense of solidarity to the perceived interests and goods of those in the community around them. They act not in isolation from these interests but with conviction that they must seek the welfare of the community in which they find themselves and that the communal welfare is at one with their own welfare. But in discovering ways to respond to these interests, Christians use the criteria given in the prophets and in Jesus Christ, and they act in the knowledge that neither their own purposes nor the competing purposes in the community will be fulfilled completely, for the covenant God has his own purposes which will be consummated.

The church-related college may find guidance for its actions and the basis for discovering its new identity in such a federal conception of human community and the governance of God. It must find its purposes and its functions not in uniqueness nor in isolation but in seeking to align itself with interests present in its constituencies and in its community. The interests to be served and the ways of serving them are to be governed by the heritage of Christian faith in the conviction that the welfare of the college is deeply involved with the welfare of its community and with the hope that its own efforts, in part self-interested though they may be, will be allied to the wider purposes of God.

74

Chapter V

EDUCATION IN AN ECUMENICAL ERA

IT IS IMPORTANT not only to raise to consciousness and examine the crisis of identity through which many of the old Christian colleges have been going but also to describe in some detail the process by which this crisis can be resolved. One essential element in such resolution is a shift away from uniqueness and toward solidarity as the central image of institutional self-understanding in Christian faith on the part of church colleges. In this way the Christian heritage ceases to be a sectarian impediment and becomes a means for uniting older and newer constituencies in a common task as well as for moving into the emerging era of ecumenism.

Solidarity with and responsibility for the world around us have implications for all areas of college operations. In this chapter and those which follow, we shall examine major spheres of concern today, indicating along the way how wrestling with these issues may be means also for dealing with problems such as student unrest and college funding. First, we shall look at the problem of diverse faiths and cultures in our time. It is an ecumenical era not only in the meeting of Catholic and Protestant Christians but also in the Marxist-Christian dialogue, in the encounter of Eastern and Western cultures, and in the competition among all the tribal ideologies in the national and global marketplaces. Second, in the succeeding chapter, the relation of higher education to society will be given attention, in particular, the danger of state control of education and the resultant importance of countervailing power in our educational system. The crucial role universities and colleges play today in shaping society and the political influence that government and industry exercise on campus will also be examined. Third, the relation of church-sponsored colleges to other parts of higher education and to the expanding spheres of educational possibility deserves attention. Fourth, the problem of governance must be explored not only in its political dimensions and as thorny issue today but also as an arena of tremendous educational significance. Fifth, the relation of social policy, the denominational college, and the churches will be explored for help in resolving the identity crisis of church institutions. And finally, the way to a new identity through responsibility to the needs of the human community will be suggested as a summary of the entire diagnosis and prescription offered here.

1. Divisive Education

Ecumenism is a fact of our time. Indeed it is one of the most important and pervasive phenomena of the twentieth century. But it is one thing to point to the development of an ecumenical spirit among persons of different backgrounds and conviction and quite another to speak of the extent to which this spirit has pervaded the institutional operation of the churches. It is not my purpose here to investigate extensively what is obviously a complex set of problems, but rather to point to crucial aspects of the present situation in ecumenical relations and to suggest the part colleges may play in transforming vague goodwill into operational ecumenism.

When one examines the issue of education for ecumenism it becomes clear at once that ecumenical hopes are not nurtured by our educational structures. The divided brethren of Christendom have entered into relationship over the past decade with good intentions and increasing goodwill, but the encounters have demonstrated that all of us have insufficient preparation for them. The blame for this lack of preparation must be placed in part on the deficient education to which we have been subjected. Our education—Protestant, Catholic, and public—has been education in institutions that have been shaped by the divided past rather than the ecumenical present. The ecumenical spirit is willing, but the institutional flesh is weak. The tasks of ecumenism are being undertaken without support from the experiences built into present-day institutional forms.

Increased goodwill and better information are a beginning, but they are not enough to support the emergent ecumenical initiatives.

It is as though an opera is being composed. The themes have been written and the overture composed, but the work of developing these themes into a complete opera has scarcely begun. And it appears that our education for harmony and orchestration has been seriously inadequate.

One of the main difficulties in developing closer relationships between Protestant Christianity and Roman Catholicism is our education. We have been educated for division and not for ecumenism. Protestant control of the common school system in this country that emerged in the nineteenth century not only placed Roman Catholics and Jews at a disadvantage but often made the public schools appear as hotbeds of sectarian instruction. Even in our own century the Protestant establishment in public education has not been completely broken. And often when it has been, it has only been because a dogmatic neutralist establishment has moved in. In a movement equally sectarian and defensive, the Roman Catholics built a system of schools parallel to that in the public arena.

The situation in higher education is scarcely different. In the nineteenth century and well into the twentieth century higher education presents to us an unhappy scene in which each denomination raced against the others to establish colleges under its own exclusive control, or worse, dominated by particular groups or viewpoints within a denomination. It is possible that more than two thousand such denominational schools were founded between the Revolution and World War I, with an appalling mortality rate, perhaps as high as 80 percent. This divisiveness and consequent weakness have had terrible consequences in church-related higher education. So-called Christian higher education in this country has usually been sectarian and designed defensively to protect the youth from the contamination of other faiths. Often it appears to protect them from education with significant breadth. Much that has gone on in the denominational colleges has been designed more to prove the opposition wrong than to advance learning or contribute well-educated citizens to the society. As a result church-related education of all sectarian stripes is for the most part uniformly inferior to that of public and private higher education. This inferiority can often be measured on a scale directly related to how great or how little control is exercised by the denomination.

An even more sweeping consequence has been that the educational

77

enterprise of all the churches has been an education for dividedness. Our church school classes, our catechetical and doctrinal instruction, and the higher education of our clergy and most devout laity, have been aimed at keeping us within the isolated confines of our own community of interpretation[1] rather than preparing us for conversation and for firm relationship with those of other faiths.

2. The New Situation: Diverse Communities of Interpretation

The ecumenical movement today forms part of a larger cultural phenomenon occurring throughout society. This twentieth-century happening may be called a meeting of communities of interpretation. By this I intend to describe the situation of contemporary man in which he finds himself emerging from the enclosed community of his ancestors within which he was protected from contradictory convictions by a wall of traditional beliefs and customs. Whether he wishes it or not, man today finds himself dragged out of the secure custody of ancestral dogmas and projected into a confusing marketplace of differing loyalties and convictions. What he has accepted before he finds questioned by others. "They" do not believe what "we" know to be true.

This meeting of communities of interpretation has many dimensions. Protestant confronts Protestant, and together they find themselves facing different convictions of the Roman Catholic community. Guilt-laden events have forced Christians to examine their relations with the Jewish community. Western religion finds itself in the presence of renascent Eastern faiths, and the entire world has been shaken by the emergence of a new faith, that of Marxist communism, which has swept around the globe with a dynamic expansion unmatched since Islam exploded out of the Arabian desert in the seventh century.

When we examine our common life more carefully, we discover more communities of interpretation in our midst. The Christian meeting with Islam is at long range, and our meeting with communism is more likely to be in headlines and in the speeches of excited politicians. There are also confrontations going on among us with the compelling convictions of Freudianism, scientism, hedonism, and

---

[1] See Josiah Royce, *The Problem of Christianity*. New York: Macmillan Co., 1913, especially vol. 2, on "community of interpretation."

other ideologies. These meetings are close at hand in popular books, plays, and on university campuses.

What the increased mobility of man has not achieved to further this meeting of communities, the mass media have continued and reinforced. By radio, newspaper, movie, and television man is instructed in detail about the variety of life and viewpoint among his fellowmen. The revolution in communications has intensified the meeting of communities of interpretation and has carried this meeting into every section of the globe and every sector of human culture. Marshall McLuhan has spoken about the world as a global village. It may be more accurate to recognize it as a global marketplace of competing commitments, conflicting loyalties, and contending faiths, that is, where the modern tribal entities meet.

Reactions to this meeting of communities in the global marketplace created by the new technological culture have been varied. The first response has been fear of the stranger and his alien views. Attempts to retreat into isolated tribal domains have been made; protective walls have been built higher and institutions devised to exclude the intruder. The American parent wants his children to be educated and goes to sacrificial efforts to make this possible. But he is deeply disturbed if his offspring emerge from school and college with expanded horizons and new ideas.

Increasingly, the efforts to maintain ethnic and ideological isolation have failed. Schools, however carefully controlled, still subvert the young. What the schools do covertly, colleges perform more openly. And what education does halfheartedly and partially, TV and travel accomplish with great affective power. Indeed, for all the thinness of its fare, television begins global orientation of persons before they have been weaned. Children and youth reach for a wider world as though by instinct and will rebel against parents who seek to restrain their growth. The vain attempt to hold off the encroachment of cultural diversity is like Canute trying to hold back the sea by kingly decree.

Upon the heels of this failure comes anxiety over the future of the heritage that has nurtured one's community. Cherished convictions and ways of life are threatened and will be destroyed by exposure to alternative views. Such anxiety represents an insecurity about the strength of conviction present in the community, doubt that the heritage is strong enough or true enough to endure in an environment of diversity, and, in itself, indicates an internal weakening of faith on the part of adherents to a tradition. When this sense of threat becomes strong, it often leads to hostility that makes its appearance through the entire spectrum of social activities. Politics becomes an arena for ethnic organization and defense. The media of communication become a battleground to undermine opposing communities and expand the influence of particular traditions. Education is turned into an instrument of religious/cultural warfare. And the past as well as our own century contains countless examples wherein competition among alternative faiths has erupted into open violence.

The same factors, however, that are producing a cultural marketplace of global scope are also making for a new situation within the differing tribes and in their relations with one another. Increased exposure to other viewpoints, working with different communities of interpretation on common problems, rubbing shoulders with persons of different convictions, have resulted in change. The fears of many have been allayed. Mutual respect and friendship have often replaced fear and hostility. It is discovered that the modern world presents the same problems to men, regardless of their ultimate perspectives. It is possible to relate to other persons and other communities on a basis of common humanity if not of identical faith.

Out of this surprising insight often comes a further development. Rather than threatening one's heritage, the meeting of diverse communities of interpretation may actually lead to mutual enrichment. Buddhists may teach Christians the deeper meanings of *Christian* compassion, or is it really *human* compassion? A Marxist philosopher such as Ernst Bloch may aid Christians to recover a biblical understanding of historical realism. The marketplace may deepen faith and compel men to become more human in their believing than isolated tribal existence could sustain.

Education at all levels can enhance this meeting of the tribes that technology has brought about. While increased knowledge and proximity are never cure-alls for the anxieties and conflicts among men, inadequate and defensive education may hinder developing relationship, and education that accepts the global marketplace and makes use of possibilities opened by technology can aid the ecumenical process.

3. Education for Ecumenism: Toward Creative Diversity

The entire spectrum of educational endeavor offers exciting opportunities for preparing persons and institutions to cope with change and deal creatively with the meeting of diverse communities of interpretation in the global marketplace. New media are being developed applicable from kindergarten through secondary school and university, useful with extension programs, church education, and community classes with adults, and capable of deepening the educational process whether it be formal classroom courses or action-oriented training in industry and community organization.

Education permeates American society and remains an important force in shaping our world. But it cannot be regarded as a panacea for all our ills. Because education can be geared to a variety of goals, both humane and inhumane, it can never displace religious faith in shaping basic values and ultimate goals or supplant political interaction as a means for allocating priorities and making community decisions. Nevertheless, education in all its forms can provide the means to illumine alternative directions, knowledge to make action more precise, and skills to use resources in moving toward societal goals. The tremendous potentiality of education should neither be exaggerated nor underestimated.

Perhaps we have painted too gloomy a picture of what is going on in the education under the auspices of churches. Certainly it is not all education for divisiveness. Many promising developments are under way in all parts of the country and in every sector of education. But there is a long way to go if our society is to be prepared adequately to deal with the rich diversity of our world or, more specifically, if the ecumenical conversations under way so auspiciously on many organizational and intellectual levels are to become operational ecumenism in the life of the laity and in the churches. Let me make a few suggestions about the kind of education that can sustain and deepen the ecumenical movement.

First, education for ecumenism must become inclusive. We must try on every level of instruction to move beyond narrowly sectarian interpretation of our own traditions and faith. Induction into the life and beliefs of our own community must not appear to involve complete rejection of Christians from other churches. Relationship to other denominations must be fostered by the study of viewpoints other than our own and by positive and continuing contacts with persons from other churches. Such education for ecumenism can be begun on the lowest levels of instruction and carried to the highest levels; and it is needed as much at the latter end of the spectrum as at the former. When Protestant and Roman Catholic theologians meet, we discover how little our own education has acquainted us with some of the major thinkers upon whom scholars in other traditions rely. If it is to be for ecumenism, our education must not only cease to be sectarian, but it must drop its defensiveness. We must move toward appreciative understanding of the best, not only of other Christians, but also of other religious traditions. This is not a plea for relaxation in regard to differences and easy agreement. Rather it is based on a considered analysis that only as we appreciatively understand what other traditions believe can we become clear as to where and why we differ. Only then will it be possible for us to discover areas of genuine agreement. Only then can we be open to the possible enrichment of our own faith that others may bring to us.

Second, education for ecumenism requires personal encounter and involvement. We shall learn for ecumenical development not only from books but also from meeting and sharing with persons of different views in common enterprises of deep concern. We must engage persons in conversation and meet them in classrooms, but we must also involve ourselves with them in community work for the common good. If one picture is worth a thousand words, then one common project where persons interact around a common concern and purpose is worth a thousand ecumenical resolutions.

Third, education for ecumenism must become multidisciplinary. Such education must broaden itself to learn from other faiths but even more it must broaden itself to learn from areas of study other than theology. Even in the movement of ecumenical theology we have engaged in a kind of theological sectarianism that seems to assume the only focus of learning where we know and serve God is theology. Education, and indeed Christianity, is far broader than doctrine. Wherever we confront man up against personal frustration and societal injustice, wherever we discover man learning about himself and his world—in biology or chemistry, in sociology or history as well as in theology and philosophy—we confront the action of God who creates, judges, and redeems.

Viewed in this way education for ecumenism may thus become

also the path from inferiority to excellence in education as it broadens us and sensitizes us to the larger working of God in his world. It will aid not only in relations among churches but also in absorbing the insights of all communities of interpretation around us. We learn in relationship with our neighbors in the global marketplace and aim toward training persons who out of the faith given them in their own tradition seek to serve the welfare and the interests of the entire human community. Though it may be many years, perhaps centuries, before great congruence of dogma emerges, we may discover that even our differences lead us toward the recognition of our common humanity and set us to solving together the problems of social justice and international conflict.

One clear result of education for ecumenism, which moves beyond sectarian defensiveness toward an inclusiveness rooted in our own faith, will be that we shall learn more about ourselves. No doubt can exist that Protestants have learned more about Luther's notion of the priesthood of all believers from the encounter with Roman Catholic ideas of the lay apostolate. On a still wider level, it is possible that Christians shall learn more of Christian compassion from the meeting with compassionate Buddhism. Certainly we have gained from contemporary Freudianism new understanding of the Augustinian and Pauline depth of human self-consciousness. In the meeting of other communities of interpretation we find ourselves open to dimensions of our own heritage that we may have missed and may even find ourselves moving toward more inclusive frames of reference in our faith.

It is here that education for ecumenism has the greatest promise. Perhaps the most significant advance to emerge from the Second Vatican Council appeared explicitly in no schema produced but rather emerged in a new openness toward a future understood to be in the hands of God rather than our own. The doctrine of the irreformability of dogma has never been the exclusive property of Roman Catholics. It has been equally as evident in Protestant denominations. But over the past decade we have learned from one another to reinterpret our dogmas of irreformability. We are learning that irreformability may mean not the unchanging repetition of past formulae but rather the unceasing search for wider conceptualizations of our faith which will not only include our own past but will enable us to relate creatively to the other traditions of faith. We are learning that the death of God in our time may mean only the changing of the little gods of our narrow past and our coming to the recognition of the God of Abraham, Isaac, and Jacob—the God of our Lord and Saviour Jesus Christ, whom we have in our partial ignorance been seeking for centuries to serve. It is this living toward the future in Jesus Christ into which ecumenical education may lead us, in which a larger learning will bring us into dialogue and ecumenical relation, not because we have denied our past but because we have seen it anew. H. Richard Niebuhr has suggested a similar pattern for ecumenicity:

> There will be no union of Catholics and Protestants until through the common memory of Jesus Christ the former repent of the sin of Peter and the latter of the sin of Luther, until Protestants acknowledge Thomas Aquinas as one of their fathers, the Inquisition as their own sin and Ignatius Loyola as one of their own Reformers, until Catholics have canonized Luther and Calvin, done repentance for Protestant Nationalism, and appropriated Schleiermacher and Barth as their theologians.[2]

Happily, this kind of ecumenism is already under way, and through the strength and spirit of Jesus Christ we must continue and expand it.

4. Models for Cooperation

From this perspective it is clear that the sectarian past is not all loss. It was a response to the situation of a time different from our own. Whether we evaluate this response as right or wrong in its own time, however, the present situation within which we must work and respond contains that past represented at least in contemporary institutional structure. The disadvantages of multiple and isolated denominational colleges are manifold, but there are creative possibilities also present, and innovative actions under way in many parts of the country indicate that certain leaders in church-related higher education are prepared to take advantage of these opportunities. Various associations of denominational institutions have come into being by means of which these institutions cooperate and

---

[2] H. Richard Niebuhr, *The Meaning of Revelation*. New York: Macmillan Co., 1941, pp. 118-119. For an understanding of Christian faith in terms of change and hope see also Jürgen Moltmann, *The Theology of Hope*. New York: Harper & Row, 1967.

strengthen each other. Such consortia are not new. Oxford and Cambridge universities comprise multiple colleges maintaining autonomy in certain respects, working closely together in other activities, and merged for still other functions. The Claremont colleges in California represent a similar pattern going back fully five decades in this country, and associations for purposes of accreditation, athletics, and fund-raising are familiar.

In parallel fashion, denominational colleges have been banding together for mutual benefits. The need for these consortia has become increasingly apparent. The impetus derives partly from economies possible through larger organizations, partly to avoid wasteful duplication, partly to achieve common tasks and goals more effectively, partly from federal legislation encouraging cooperation, and partly to take advantage of the enrichment that the interaction of diverse institutions produces. The cooperative patterns range from loose associations for very specific purpose to tightly binding legal consortia.[3]

One example of such innovation is the grouping of denominational colleges known as the Associated Colleges of Central Kansas.[4] In an era of highways and automobiles, these once-isolated colleges found themselves increasingly close to one another. Member colleges of ACCK are Bethany College, Bethel College, Kansas Wesleyan, McPherson College, Sterling College, and Tabor College. Denominational affiliation includes: Church of the Brethren, Mennonite Brethren, Mennonite, United Methodist, Lutheran, and United Presbyterian. No college is farther than forty miles from McPherson, Kansas, the location of McPherson College. In 1900, geographical distance separated them. Today they are close neighbors. In 1900, sectarian differences provided chasms among them that are no longer of overwhelming importance.

Loose association and increasing joint meetings among these col-

---

[3] See Eldon L. Johnson, "Consortia in Higher Education," *Educational Record*, Fall, 1967; Frampton Davis, "Developing Colleges through Interinstitutional Cooperation," *Educational Record*, Fall, 1967; Eldon L. Johnson, "New Collegiate Options through Joint Action," *Liberal Education*, March, 1968; and Pressley C. McCoy, "The Forms of Interinstitutional Cooperation," *Liberal Education*, March, 1968.

[4] This account is heavily dependent on a paper by President Paul W. Renich, of Kansas Wesleyan, "Consortia: A Case Study of Associated Colleges of Central Kansas," mimeographed.

leges go back several decades. By 1964, the need for closer association became clear, and talks were started that led first to a cooperative program in non-Western cultures in 1964 and then to the organization of ACCK in 1966. ACCK is an incorporated entity to which each of the six colleges has ceded a portion of its autonomy. The new corporation, which can acquire property, borrow money, grant certificates and diplomas, and confer degrees, is financed partly by funds from the colleges and partly by grants primarily from the Department of Health, Education, and Welfare.[5] The association has its own executive, and joint efforts have been undertaken in a common calendar, library services, administrative and business functions, data processing, faculty development and visiting scholars, educational policy, international programs, science facilities, instruction, and communications. By this joint action, these colleges have not only improved the use of their resources but also have made a much wider range of support available and have strengthened the church-related college system of Kansas. It can be done—even today.

The Central States College Association and the Associated Colleges of the Midwest offer further examples. These colleges are widely dispersed geographically compared with the group in Kansas. Nevertheless, they are undertaking joint planning, exchange of students, common programs abroad in urban areas, and cooperative use of faculty. In contrast to the Kansas group, which so far contains only Protestant colleges, these groups contain Roman Catholic and private colleges as members and therefore add to the diversity of resources and perspectives.

In Berkeley, California, the Graduate Theological Union provides

---

[5] It appears probable that the courts will support federal grants for non-sectarian uses to church-related colleges, though the character and limits of such grants must be clarified further in specific congressional acts and court decisions. Cf. "Church-College Grants Upheld by U.S. Court," *The Chronicle of Higher Education*, vol. 4, no. 25, March 30, 1970, pp. 1, 2; and "Court's Ruling on Federal Grants to Church Colleges," ibid., p. 2. In part this ruling of a three-judge federal panel asserts: "Indeed the legislative history is quite conclusive that Congress intended to make the benefits of the [Higher Education Facilities Act of 1963] available to church-related colleges and universities. . . . In short, here we find no conflict between preservation of religious freedom and provision of higher education. Without both, we may end up with neither." Further articulation of the limits of federal aid occurred in Tilton v. Richardson (1971); see "Triumph Turns to Concern as Church-College Leaders Weigh Implications of Supreme Court Decisions," *The Chronicle of Higher Education*, August 2, 1971, pp. 1, 3.

another model for cooperation. Over the past century a dozen denominational seminaries were founded in the San Francisco Bay Area. Most of them were intentionally isolated from one another and from the university environment. Protestant sectarian institutions were paralleled by the insularity of seminaries affiliated with Roman Catholic orders. Now six Protestant and three Roman Catholic seminaries are integrally related for doctoral work in theology and are finding increasing areas of cooperation on the seminary level. All are moving out of their isolation toward close involvement with the University of California, Berkeley. Those that were geographically isolated are moving their operations to Berkeley in order to be close to one another and to the stimulating environment of a major university. The combining of faculties, libraries, and student bodies has transformed Berkeley into one of the major theological centers of the world. This development has its counterparts in theological consortia in all parts of the country.

In these examples it may be seen that the sectarian pattern of church-related higher education may become an important resource for ecumenical education as denominational colleges wrestle with the problems of the present rather than being only a troublesome disadvantage inherited from the nineteenth century. Through various cooperative arrangements denominational colleges may relate instructional programs, exchange students, combine faculty resources, construct joint facilities, merge libraries or provide easy exchange of books, and initiate cooperative action in regard to urban education, social justice, and international involvement.

In the process of such cooperation, church-related institutions may achieve something even more important than organizational efficiency and financial saving. They may demonstrate the significance of diversity and dissent, disagreement and conflict, as important elements in a creative scheme of higher education. In a contemporary situation in which the meeting of communities of interpretation is an inescapable fact of our common life, only education that comprises a variety of views and teaches in its practice the creative potential in such diversity can be called either realistic or adequate preparation for living in today's world. Under ideological and financial pressure, public colleges and universities have often limited the dissent and diversity of perspectives presented on campus. Ecumenical cooperation of denominational institutions may thus strengthen elements in danger of being seriously weakened in contemporary higher education.

Such cooperation, designed as a contribution to educational process, may well be motivated by the biblical Christian heritage. Certainly Jeremiah was calling for the recognition of conflict and diversity when he decried, "Peace, peace, when there is no peace." And Paul may be interpreted in support of such an enterprise when he said that in Christ there is neither Jew nor Gentile, neither Greek nor barbarian, when he spoke of Christ as tearing down the walls that divide men and uniting all things in himself. Indeed, the history of Christianity may be seen as a series of encounters with conflicting perspectives, encounters that were not rejected but which led instead to serious meeting and appropriation from supposed opponents. Such ability to appropriate and be transformed by conflict is a significant clue to the strength of the Hebrew-Christian movement. The meeting with and appropriation from the mystery religions and Greek philosophy provide illustrations of the way Christianity has grown in power by ever increasing comprehensiveness. Christian skepticism has never been directed only at other views of the world but also at the adequacy of its own conceptualizations or actions as fully expressive of Christian faith. Michael Polanyi provides an important insight for Christian theology and education when he suggests that the Christian understanding of God is not a static dogma but rather a heuristic impulse to break through and move beyond accepted conceptual frameworks.[6] The sectarian past may thus provide the basis for important contributions to the public present of American higher education and a pattern for moving into a wider, more human future.

---

[6] Cf. Michael Polanyi, *Personal Knowledge*. Chicago: University of Chicago Press, 1958.

Chapter VI

CHURCH, STATE, AND SOCIETY

THE GREAT differences of sponsorship, type, and function among American colleges and universities may deceive the partially informed into believing that institutions of higher education represent wide diversity in all respects. Perceptive observers have for some time been questioning this conventional opinion. Their views find increasing support from research. Warren Bryan Martin of the Center for Research and Development in Higher Education, Berkeley, completed in 1969 an Institutional Character Study of eight colleges and universities in different parts of the nation. The report is both illuminating and disturbing. Rather than finding change toward greater diversity in values and norms, in operational styles and results, Martin located little concrete evidence of the development or encouragement of such diversity.[1]

The issue is not new. For example, David Riesman in the fifties spoke of "the tendency among college administrations and faculties towards isomorphism, towards taking each other as models rather than developing new and risky forms." [2] The tendencies toward isomorphism have not decreased; indeed they are probably stronger. What Martin has done is to delineate with greater precision the areas of conformity that obvious patterns of diversity conceal from most observers. Further in the past, churches often tried to impose

[1] Warren Bryan Martin, *Conformity: standards and change in higher education*. San Francisco: Jossey-Bass, 1969, p. 215.

[2] David Riesman, *Constraint and Variety in American Education*. Garden City, New York: Doubleday, 1958, p. 10.

doctrinal authority on higher education and thereby restrict diversity of opinion. Isomorphism can derive from general societal pressures as the public elementary and secondary schools often illustrate. A primary source of pressure toward conformity today may come from the state.

Whatever the source, isomorphism constitutes a deadly threat to higher education. One may ask whether "higher" education is possible where pressures toward conformity in basic values and goals prevail. In our society elementary, secondary, and higher education have become names for educational institutions. But these stages are represented as functions, institutionalized in varying degrees, in any society. Persons must develop the basic, elementary ability for understanding and communicating within the complex system of meaning that constitutes a culture. A secondary level of education provides skills for performing needed functions within society. And a higher level involves conscious study of the purposes and values of the culture in forming and shaping the society and, further, critical evaluation and reshaping of that culture to deal with new circumstances. All three levels are necessary for continuing, operating, and developing a society.

To the extent that colleges are conformist and uncritical with regard to cultural values and purposes a crucial function of higher education is missing. Isomorphism diminishes and could lead effectively to the elimination of this function.

Consideration of the church college in relation to state and society requires this expanded context rather than resolving the problem into the legal issue of church and state. We must examine the development of education, the peril of state dominance, the importance of diversity and countervailing power in education, and the possibilities existing beyond either conformity or mere competition among church-related and public higher education.

1. The Great Experiment

The dilemma confronting the church-related college between its sectarian past and public present appears sharply when one considers the consequence of the entrance on a massive scale of the states and the federal government into higher education. An area that was once virtually monopolized by ecclesiastical and private control has now come largely under the dominance of government agencies at the district, state, and federal levels. The need for and character of a new identity on the part of the church-related college come into focus when one considers the problem of its relation to state-supported higher education.

Let us first take a brief look at what has occurred. Sometime during the latter part of the nineteenth century the United States embarked upon what must be regarded as a great experiment in universal education. In retrospect this launching of a movement to provide education for everyone may come to be regarded as the facet of American society with even greater long-range significance for global society than our industrial development and the achievement of world political leadership. Indeed, these latter attainments would probably have been impossible apart from the program of mass education that accompanied them. And the success or failure of our efforts at international leadership may be determined by how well we carry out the ambitious educational task that our society has set for itself or, put in a more ominous mood, how rapidly our education can find ways to overcome our tragic immaturity in international relations.

It must be called the great experiment because no society in the short history of mankind had attempted it before. Previously education beyond elementary levels has been reserved for special groups—for ecclesiastical, social, and intellectual elites. America decided to apply the same democratic tendencies inherent in our society since colonial days to the sphere of education. First, elementary education was extended and made virtually universal. Then secondary education was expanded and made available to all. And over the past century the same democratic notions have been applied to higher education. In 1869, only one of every 1,927 persons of college age was enrolled in an institution of higher education. By 1946, better than one in five was enrolled, and by the late sixties the figure was almost one in every two. Because the resources were not available to churches and private institutions to carry out this far-reaching conception, and indeed because much higher education had been designed to preserve aristocratic and ecclesiastical privilege, the state undertook the gigantic task of financing the great experiment.

As a result, our entire system of education has undergone sweeping changes. Rather than being controlled by local and special-interest communities, schools have come under the increasing control of public agencies on regional, state, and national levels. In elementary and secondary education only the Roman Catholic Church has made extensive efforts to keep control of the educational process within a particular denomination, and this effort has become increasingly costly and has met with declining success. In higher education there has been a determined and extensive effort also by non-Catholics to maintain colleges related to church agencies. Here also a crisis of resources has been emerging relentlessly.

Amazing consequences of the great experiment are already in evidence. More obvious changes are the tremendous growth in the educational establishment, the great increase in amounts expended on education, the huge growth in numbers of students at all levels, and the multiplication of functions performed by the educational systems. There are also less obvious changes. A vast reservoir of trained personnel has been made available to undergird the expansion of American society. Never before has a social group taken possession of a wilderness, developed its industry, acquired a culture, and achieved global hegemony so rapidly as has the United States. Technical mastery, advanced research, and mass-produced innovation have become the hallmarks of contemporary America. Through our diversified educational system we have tapped the abilities of middle and lower socioeconomic groups largely excluded from opportunity and leadership in older systems. Paths have been opened to the "late bloomers" and to the socially disadvantaged. Where we are yet failing to absorb all potential resources, strong pressures to democratize further push us forward irresistibly. The G.I. Bill after World War II provided a giant step toward universal higher education, and programs to widen opportunities for the socially disadvantaged and ethnic minorities continue to multiply. So rapidly have we developed and such close continuity with Western culture have we maintained, we usually forget that in the eyes of Europe we are an upstart civilization scarcely out of colonial and frontier conditions.

The great experiment has already produced amazing results, but even vaster implications may lie hidden in the future if we can achieve political maturity to match our technical competence with sufficient speed to prevent our self-destruction. Already our advances have led the Soviet Union rapidly toward imitation of our system of universal education, and even the old and respected systems of Western Europe are being forced to reshape their aristocratic patterns by the pressure of American and Russian achievements. Colleges and universities now comprise one of the greatest resources of American society. As James A. Perkins has put it, ". . . higher education is now the proper concern of every man who wishes his country well." [3]

Though they have become less sectarian, church-related colleges have tended to remain tied to particular groups and classes throughout this period of transition. Now the changes in American expectations of higher education are forcing these institutions into a situation of crisis—a situation containing both peril to their existence and opportunity to reconceive their destiny. The symptoms appear most clearly in the financial pinch and in the competition for faculty and students. But the real challenge before the church-related college is to join more fully in the great experiment or perish.

2. Perils of State Dominance

The massive shift from elite to democratic conceptions of education and the launching of the great experiment in America have yielded enormous advantages for American society, but certain dangers have also accompanied the transition. To put the change in another way: we have moved from a situation in which society, through various communities, local and intentional, was the sponsor of education, to a situation in which the state is now dominant. The various components of American society with all their diversity once presided over the communication of our cultural tradition through control of the educational media. Now the state increasingly provides the context in which culture is communicated. This way of putting the matter suggests its more ominous possibilities. State sponsorship could lead from dominance to control of education and from control to totalitarian indoctrination.

The peril of state dominance in education has been increasing throughout this century but has become sufficiently obvious only in recent years to evoke widespread concern. In a fascinating and almost unique area of agreement, this concern comes from both left and right on the political spectrum. Criticism of the trend toward state control is made by social liberals on the grounds that an educa-

---

[3] James A. Perkins, *The University in Transition*. Princeton: Princeton University Press, 1966, p. 89.

tional system subservient to the faction holding political office may become an instrument for achieving totalitarian power and transforming our republic into a dictatorship. Opposition from the right derives from a parallel suspicion of centralized government, suspicion rooted in the laissez-faire liberalism of an earlier era. Conservatives today object to the state's taking over the functions of communicating culture, functions previously controlled by diverse communities, some locally or ideologically defined, others defined by religious faith or social status. When we consider that public control of education has tended to overcome parochial forms of discrimination and provided increased financing and quality, the socially conscious liberals of today have good reason to welcome the shift that has taken place. Old-style liberals, who play conservative roles today, have many reservations about this democratic leveling. But when the new liberals become aware of the possibilities of state control of education, of indoctrinating the young in a nationalistic cultus that identifies patriotism with the endorsement of prevailing national policies, then they begin to recognize the perils implicit in the situation for denying the right of dissent and diminishing the protection of minority points of view. And the conservatives, while opposing centralized control, may welcome the enforcement of traditional values.

Regardless of the strange alliances this situation may sometimes create, it is clear that ecclesiastical authority is no longer a major threat to freedom of opinion and education. Today, whether through control of educational media, oppressive use of police power, or the investigative authority of the F.B.I., whether through the force of available funds or the covert influences of the C.I.A., the state has become the most significant threat to freedom and diversity in America.

As long ago as 1949, Horace M. Kallen expressed the view that education had become a major vehicle for indoctrination and authoritarianism. "Teaching," he wrote, "is made the art of wearing intellectual blinkers. . . . School administrations are dictatorships; that student self-government is a sham and a pretense. . . . In sum, education . . . is indoctrination in a dated grammar of assent." [4] And

---

[4] Horace M. Kallen, *The Education of Free Man, An Essay Towards a Philosophy of Education for America.* New York: Farrar, Straus, 1949, pp. 145, 146.

this was in the era before Senator Joseph McCarthy rose to power and cast his spell over anxious middle America.

Alliance between left and right does not always appear so benign as when both oppose control of education by big-brother government. Sometimes it has more ominous overtones. At few points in the sixties did the coalition of left and right appear more clearly or more dangerously than in the blatant political firing in January, 1967, of President Clark Kerr by the regents of the University of California. It took place less than three weeks after Ronald Reagan had been inaugurated as governor of California and represented his policy, consistently stressed during his campaign and also during his tenure in office to use higher education for his own political purposes. The abrupt decision to dismiss Kerr meant capitulation on the part of the regents to political pressure from the right-wing vultures, who hovered around the university hopefully from the time of the Free Speech Movement in 1964, and from left-wing extremists and the hard-core radicals among the students, who had long denounced Kerr. The action of the regents raised grave issues about the relation of the state to higher education.

Can the state support higher education of excellence? A great college or university must be able to entertain diverse and even socially unpopular views. Wide-ranging discussion in a context of intellectual check and balance is the rich seed bed of creativity. Higher education cannot perform its crucial functions of criticism and innovation, even with reference to cherished social goals and values, if the heavy hand of state repression attempts to control its life. In a speech the year after his dismissal, Clark Kerr himself raised the issue of the danger to freedom and creativity in higher education from the state. If the state tries to repress diverse views and punish all who hold them, rather than maintain an open marketplace of opinion, protect its citizens from violence, and carry out policies within constitutional limits, then it dooms the society to destruction through failure to let it grow and change, and it increases the likelihood of disorder and even revolution, as the history of tyranny demonstrates.

But before we push the panic button in regard to the perils of state dominance in public education, we should remember that neither the state nor federal government has exerted as much pressure as might be expected when one considers the money they have provided for colleges and universities. The dangerous policies of Ronald Reagan have not prevailed generally. Greater than external pressures from state or federal sources is the eager capitulation of faculty and administrations to the offer of funds to support research. Instead of critical review of projects offered, colleges and universities have sought state subsidies and fought over them.

The threat to higher education from the state is real. But it has usually appeared in the distortion of purpose through funds eagerly sought by educators rather than in direct pressure from government. And even more important, perhaps, is the imitative, isomorphic tendency that higher education has acquired to a deplorable degree from the conformist elements in our society. It is to this peril present within the promise of the great experiment that church-related higher education must address itself in any search for a new identity that will contribute creatively to the common good of our society and the global culture of which it is part.

3. Isomorphism and Countervalence in a Higher Education System

In this situation of peril and opportunity, church-related and private colleges have important functions to perform within the total higher educational system of the society. On the one hand, it is high time for these colleges to take more decisive action toward joining the great experiment, finding more effective ways to break out of the "special-interest" ideology that has informed their past and to make greater contributions to the widening movement of universal education on regional, national, and global levels. On the other hand, it is important to recognize that we need private and church-related higher education to provide alternatives to the tendencies toward a deadly educational sameness in a system of higher education that on the surface appears to be diverse.

The pressures to join the worldwide movement toward universal education derive from so many quarters today that it may appear superfluous to emphasize it. What was a great experiment has been sufficiently successful both in attainment and in projecting to peoples in all parts of the world hope for a better future so as to make the expansion and democratization of education a mounting tide. The urgency of the task, however, may go unrecognized. The growth in world population, the "revolution of rising expectations" that increases the demand for more education, and the inertia of educational and societal leadership create a situation of frustrated hopes that has led to unrest and frequent violence in every country and in virtually every institution of higher learning in the world. Leaders either in government or on campus who think repressive measures can solve the problems of peoples determined to achieve greater control over their own destinies will find it impossible to halt the relentlessly advancing waves of human liberation. Short-run political interests may be served but not the cause of humankind nor of societal harmony. In the United States repressive policies are setting frustrated middle-class whites against frustrated black, brown, red, and youth minorities. The social disorder will increase until the determined hopes of these minorities are met with solutions to problems rather than with empty rhetoric and police brutality. The interests of frustrated middle America and frustrated minority America are similar. Strong leadership in the political and educational arenas is needed to weld these apparently opposing groups into coalitions against those who try to retain power and societal benefits in the hands of elitist groups.

At the same time, when the pressures of state money force higher education toward bland isomorphism, not only in curriculum but more basically in interests served, in goals set, and in commitments made, there is a threat to excellence, however interpreted, and a continuing danger that less powerful groups in society will not find their needs met. In such a situation, variety of control and diversity of function are not simply to be tolerated nor even welcomed; most emphatically, they must be cultivated.

The problems of underdeveloped societies and societal groups are exacerbated when patterns of admission, curriculum, and decision-making in sectors of higher education are geared to older prestige structures and social purposes.[5] Various minorities, awakened to hope but frustrated by inadequate educational channels for actualizing their aspirations, will seek to force colleges and universities to open up new programs related to their needs. But, where resistance to change rather than informed cooperation meets these efforts, then the results may well be either confrontation and violence or

---

[5] For a discussion of the complexities of educational development see Philip H. Coombs, *The World Educational Crisis: A Systems Analysis*. New York: Oxford University Press, 1968.

the reluctant acquiescence to curricular additions that are ill-advised and do not meet real needs.

Church-related colleges can play a significant role within higher education by widening the arena of values and commitments and by responding creatively to the needs of diverse constituencies present around them. It is not necessary to have idealistic illusions about these colleges or to make spurious claims to their uniqueness in order to affirm the need for diverse institutions, responding to the needs of diverse constituencies, having diverse values and commitments, with diverse sources of support, in order to serve as countervailing forces to the monolithic tendencies of public higher education.

Or again, certain elements in our society seem increasingly intent upon inculcating narrow, chauvinistic values. To counterbalance these forces diversity must be prized highly—for the sake of education worthy of the name, for the sake of American society and its future, and for the longer heritage of the Judeo-Christian faith. The greatest enemy of education, as of democracy, is easy agreement and coerced consent. Diversity of viewpoint is essential in learning, and a clash of opinions is the core of education in critical thinking. Enforced orthodoxies may be memorized, but they do not educe innovative reflection. Consensual training, whether in a classroom, on a campus, or within a total educational system, feeds on rote learning, but only dissensual processes and conflicting perspectives lift learning above dull routine toward genuine education.

Despite the lessons of history and the insights of educational psychology, one still finds mediocre administrators and timid professors, threatened by controversy and fearful of dissent, striving to maintain false and therefore dangerous harmonies. Not only are unpopular opinions excluded because their presence might disturb wealthy constituencies, but also differing views are often excluded because insecure academicians feel inadequate in the presence of complexity.

Defense of diversity and dissent in the name of educational excellence must be made before every constituency from which a college hopes to receive support. Such defense need not be based on the liberal optimism that a free marketplace of viewpoints will inevitably produce truth. Instead, it might better be rooted in the Christian and democratic convictions that all power, whether in the realm of ideas or politics, must be limited by counterpower, that partial views need the countervailing thrust of other views. Church-related colleges may enrich their educational climate as well as serve a useful role in the wider context of American higher education by cultivating dissent in their processes of learning and by a critical pluralism of societal values.[6]

Such diversity is needed also for the continuing flexibility and growth of American society. Certainly in our century, a static society is a dying society. Given the platitudinous character of that insight, it is amazing to see those who want American society to be chained to the values and techniques of the past. Americanism reduced to dogmas drawn from our romanticized perception of our grand-fathers' day is true neither to the dynamic character of our heritage nor to the innovative courage of our grandfathers. Such perverse Americanism is comparable to the process of "learning by imprint-ing" observed by Lorenz among goslings.

> Whatever a gosling . . . first sees in the hours after hatching, be it bird, beast or man, the gosling will follow as it normally would follow its mother. . . . However persistent is the fixation was shown in another experiment in which the first thing presented to the eyes of a budgereegah remained forever its only object of attachment and its days of courtship were spent in trying to make love to a ping-pong ball.[7]

Karl Deutsch applies the lesson to human groups.

> Cultures or states, ever since the days of the Spartans, have often put taboos or legal prohibitions in the way of all messages that might change their previously determined patterns of behavior. Modern nations, governments, or political parties in war or peace may strive to perpetuate their policies by blocking all incompatible experiences from the life of their community through all means at their disposal—legislation, indoctrination, pressure, censorship, police, or propaganda . . . [thus restricting] the subsequent experi-ences of that group and its members.[8]

---

[6] See Frank Pinner, "The Crisis of the State Universities: Analysis and Rem-edies," in R. Nevitt Sanford (ed.), *The American College*. New York: Wiley, 1962, pp. 940-971.

[7] W. Grey Walter, *The Living Brain*. New York: Norton, 1953, p. 136.

[8] Karl W. Deutsch, *The Nerves of Government: Models of Political Com-munication and Control*. New York: Free Press, 1966, p. 107.

Excessive isomorphism does not preserve the past of a society save as a dead body is preserved in formaldehyde. A living society requires diversity of commitments, values, and purposes in order to make room for and encourage the recognition of the innovation without which the past becomes a noose and the changing present a scaffold trapdoor into oblivion.

Though church-related and private institutions may perform this countervailing function by their very existence, they may find it possible to play an even more active and vital role. With their relative independence of pressures from political bodies, these colleges may find new educational patterns in which to serve as pioneers for higher education and for the larger society. Moving creatively beyond the isomorphic tendencies present in both public and non-public higher education, Florida Presbyterian College (now Eckerd College) blazed trails in interdisciplinary curriculum construction and in classroom design, and the University of the Pacific opened up the possibilities of cluster colleges. In similar fashion, Lewis and Clark College developed an innovative program in international education, preparing students better for living in our multicultured world. Some colleges have worked in the area of social witness, recruiting from minority groups, developing programs concerned with a better environment, and leading students into work in urban ghettos on the relentlessly mounting problems of our cities. Other colleges might find similar opportunities in the national division over the Indo-Chinese war and civil rights.

If church-related colleges are to play such a role, they must undergo a radical rethinking of their purposes and functions. They must move toward discovering a new identity for themselves in the changing scene of contemporary America.

4. Beyond Conformity and Competition

James A. Perkins has observed that the rigidity into which German and English patterns of higher education have fallen during this century has inhibited continuing creativity within those European systems. They "are now frozen in the organizational concrete of the German institute and the English college. Now that German, and particularly English, social and economic development both demand and need new and more rounded orientation in higher education, the universities face a major upheaval if they are to respond." [9] Quite clearly, parallel dangers exist at present in American higher education. If we are to escape ossification, then it is necessary for colleges and universities to move quite self-consciously beyond isomorphism and conformity. There are contributions to be made today simply in being different, and the contributions will be even more significant if the difference is based upon the discovery of important needs and interests in the society around and moving creatively in response.

To the extent that colleges and universities insist upon trying to be like one another, they inevitably increase the competition for the limited number of students whose interests correspond as well as for the funds available to perform the functions selected. If all colleges attempt to conform, for example, exclusively to the liberal arts model, then the competition for the students who want, who are capable of, and who can afford this kind of liberal arts education will become destructively intense.

To meet the variety of valid interests and to secure support from diverse donors, it is essential that colleges find different missions within which to work out their roles and functions. The University of the Pacific in Stockton, California, borrowing from the Oxford pattern of different colleges but adapting it to the American environment, developed the notion that each college might have a different mission and educational pattern. Small colleges within a university context answered the demands of students for more personal environment of learning and permitted various types of excellence to be pursued not possible on a mass basis. It also meant that different publics and different needs could be served. At the same time, greater efficiency was achieved by having many functions to be performed on a centralized basis by the university. It is not surprising that the idea has been picked up and replicated with modifications all over the nation.

Finding different purposes to pursue, however, will make a contribution to American higher education not only because it breaks the deadly grip of conformity but also because it opens up the possibility for moving beyond direct competition. Church-related higher

---

[9] James A. Perkins, *The University in Transition*. Princeton: Princeton University Press, 1966, p. 14.

education cannot, in most instances, compete with the public sectors throughout the entire spectrum of educational programs. The fantastic proliferation of functions in American education, combined with the ruinously increasing costs of operation, makes it impossible for the majority of church and private colleges to compete successfully with their public counterparts. Ample resources are simply not available to them. In this situation the temptation is strong for churches to retreat and abandon their efforts in higher education. Rationalizations are easy. After all, isn't it the task of the churches to perform functions society at large does not recognize as its responsibility and to abandon these operations once society takes them over? One can draw from this view the conclusion that the time has come for the entire task of higher education to be turned over to public agencies.

When one considers, however, the need for diversity, just the opposite conclusion can be drawn. It is indeed inappropriate for church-related colleges to attempt direct competition with public institutions. Instead, the churches should use their resources to make contributions that public schools are not making either because of societal restrictions or the pressure of public funding. A particular college should look around at its community, at its constituencies, at the needs and interests present, and discover its identity through purposes and functions that add new dimensions or fill gaps in the educational spectrum. It should move in this direction not with the hope of finding roles that cannot be performed by public higher education but rather as tasks that are not being carried out and are worth doing. Some roles will require pioneering. Others will require providing special opportunities for disadvantaged groups. Still others may be conventional but carried out in innovative ways.

In these and other ways church-related higher education is called to move beyond competition and try out new patterns. For example, a church-related college might explore moving into the context of a public university and becoming a cluster college, in part sharing the educational resources of the university and in part performing separate curricular functions. Denominational theological seminaries are already moving in this direction. As several seminaries move into the orbit of the same university, they derive the benefits both of the university context and of ecumenical relationships. A model for operation at the undergraduate level is available at Waterloo University in Canada. The modest efforts in this direction in the United States have not been successful, but the experiment has really not been tried with enough imagination and vigor. The task of the church in higher education has not been completed. But the church-related college today must move beyond the functions of the past and respond to the possibilities lying beyond conformity and competition.

Chapter VII

NEW DIMENSIONS
IN HIGHER EDUCATION

WE HAVE SPOKEN of the crisis of identity presently afflicting church-related colleges, and have suggested that one way to describe this is as a situation in which these colleges are caught between their sectarian past and the demands of a public present. Remnants of the sectarian past are visible in the persistent illusions about the past of church-sponsored institutions of higher education, in the seeking for a spurious uniqueness that would provide functions for church-related colleges not possible for those operating in the public sphere, and in a strange distortion of Christian faith that justifies a retreat from serving the common good. On the other hand, we have sought to show that the affiliations and convictions resulting from the sectarian past are not without their value as church-related colleges discover new identities for themselves in the public present. Ecumenical cooperation offers opportunities for education that prepare persons for living creatively in the diverse culture of our globe. In addition, church sponsorship may serve as an alternative power in an educational marketplace increasingly dominated by the state and characterized by mediocre imitation.

Explaining how church-related higher education can move beyond conformity and competition and contribute to the public present requires that we deal with educational possibilities available not only to colleges and universities sponsored by churches but to all higher education. To put it differently, we must now deal with the potentialities of church-related colleges not as they have a sectarian past but as they are part of the public present of education in the United States.

What we shall say now is, for the most part, as applicable to public and private colleges and universities as to church-related institutions. The perspective will remain within the Judeo-Christian faith but in the way suggested in chapter 4, which requires us to address issues of *human* concern rather than of sectarian interest. As has been true all along, illustrations will be more readily applicable to colleges than to universities, though there are also implications for universities. We shall examine a task of higher education that is emerging with increasing clarity today: education for moral concern, critical evaluation, and social responsibility. Later, we shall deal with the meaning of this moral dimension in higher education for internal governance and social policy.

1. Tasks of the Academy

As stated by William Rainey Harper, and illustrated in the University of Chicago, the tasks of higher education may be enumerated as instruction, research, and extension. Many institutions today are still organized around these activities. But times have been changing, and James A. Perkins has recently enumerated the basic functions of higher education somewhat differently: the acquisition, transmission, and application of knowledge.[1] In a perceptive book on which I shall draw later, John D. Millett sees the tasks of higher education as preserving, transmitting, and advancing knowledge.[2] Whether one prefers the formulation of Harper, Perkins, or Millett, the tasks to which they direct our attention are obviously central. The issue being raised today by educators, especially younger professors, by students in their protests and movements for educational reform, and by many thoughtful public leaders, is whether these tasks are an adequate description of what higher education must do. Our most troublesome problems now are not in carrying out the functions named. All are well developed, well financed, and growing. There is an increasing demand that higher education be more than a "knowledge factory and storehouse."

---

[1] James A. Perkins, *The University in Transition*. Princeton: Princeton University Press, 1966.

[2] John D. Millett, *The Academic Community: An Essay on Organization*. New York: McGraw-Hill, 1962.

Much more puzzling and much more urgent than the transmission and advancement of knowledge is the problem: *how to use the vast knowledge, technology, and power of our society responsibly.* We are strong and confident when it comes to the matter of acquiring knowledge. We have taken vast strides in learning not only to transmit knowledge but to store it in huge computer banks for rapid retrieval. We have moved with vigor and imagination to apply our knowledge to increasing ranges of human life. In all these functions, innovation and progressive improvement have become the American way.

We are weak not in these areas but in the arenas of moral decision. We lack evaluative criteria for guiding our efforts. Learned and skillful as we are, we are uncertain what knowledge is worth acquiring. Even as our computers have become more complex, we become less certain which data are really important and therefore worth storing and transmitting. With all our technology, we have become increasingly aware of our ineptitude when it comes to applying all that we know for the benefit of mankind or to put it more modestly, so we shall not destroy mankind, ourselves included. As some would put it: we have knowledge but lack wisdom.

In *The Uses of the University,* Clark Kerr provides a brilliant analysis of the huge university complex that increasingly is shaping our society. Yet the book contains no clear vision for directing the multiversity. Like Topsy, it just grows, and the chief administrator is to be merely a mediator among the competing forces that determine its development. Kerr rejects David Riesman's accusation that leading institutions of higher learning are directionless. He writes:

> The fact is that they are not directionless; they have been moving in clear directions and with considerable speed. . . . But these directions have not been set as much by the university's visions of its destiny as by the external environment, including the federal government, the foundations, the surrounding and sometimes engulfing industry.[3]

But Kerr suggests no solution except mediation: "The process cannot be stopped. . . . It remains to adapt." [4] By inadvertence and omission,

---

[3] Clark Kerr, *The Uses of the University.* Cambridge, Massachusetts: Harvard University Press, 1963, p. 122.

[4] Ibid., p. 124.

Kerr directs our attention to a serious inadequacy at the very center of higher education. We build more powerful vehicles for ourselves but become less certain about our abilities to steer them. Higher education will do no more than speed us on the way to catastrophe unless we can, as Roger Heyns has insisted, "widen the arena of moral discourse" on campus and in society.

Michael Polanyi says we are often least serious about what is most important. That is clearly the case when we consider the functions of higher education. We have been desperately serious about developing our technology. But we have allocated few of our resources to developing ways to train for moral decision. Some would hold that such training is impossible and therefore investigation would be futile. Others would hold that it is simply "caught" from parents, peers, and teachers. As a result, we transmit masses of specialized knowledge but do not take seriously education of the whole person. There are many today who believe higher education is seriously deficient at this point and that the three functions of Harper, Perkins, and Millett are impressive but not adequate. There is a growing number of educators and citizens who believe we must seek for new dimensions in our educational processes.

2. A Fourth Dimension

Rather than saying there is another function or task of higher education separable from the other three, it may be better to speak of a fourth dimension in higher education, a dimension that must be present in all a college or university undertakes. This dimension requires not so much adding new subject matter as providing for ethical inquiry and critical evaluation in every area of study. Adding more courses will not do the job. Nor will including the study of religion in the curriculum necessarily add this dimension. Religion can also be taught in terms of academic noninvolvement and personal sterility, just as math or sociology or literature. What is required is commitment, reflection, and action in classroom, in laboratory, and in arenas of human relationship on campus and in society. The fourth dimension does not add additional information but rather sharpens the sense of moral responsibility.

Higher education may be defined as any education beyond secondary school. If this is all, then college and university really mean more education rather than higher education. Undoubtedly much that goes on in colleges and universities qualifies as merely more of the same. If the education that goes on within the college is to qualify as "higher," then it must give constant attention to the dimension that includes critical evaluation, balanced judgment, and moral responsibility. This fourth dimension, which defines higher education and without which there can be no responsible decisions for transmitting, advancing, or applying knowledge, cannot be taught or learned in isolation from the entire process of living. It must be a deliberately cultivated dimension of education considered as a whole. Undoubtedly it was education considered only as the acquisition, transmission, and application of knowledge that produced the condition of which Ralph Waldo Emerson was critical. "The state of society is one in which the members have suffered amputation from the trunk, and strut about so many walking monsters—a good finger, a neck, a stomach, an elbow, but never a man." By exposing students to specialized disciplines, isolated from one another and from human problems, colleges and universities have developed well-trained "Frankensteins," beings with great power but no soul. When students have protested against such dehumanized education, college leaders have more often called the police than faced the issue of educational reform.

Education with this fourth dimension requires the simple but profound and often forgotten insight that in the educational process we are dealing only secondarily with knowledge and primarily with human beings. When a college or a university begins to conceive its central task as the advancement of learning or passing on the tradition of the past to the upcoming generation, or applying the knowledge acquired to the problems of society, then it is engaging in a fit of academic absentmindedness in which it forgets that the central task is educating and preparing persons for responsible roles in relation to their fellow human beings. Knowledge remains human only when it is kept within the personal context of goals, interests, and moral process. Higher education conceived in this way cannot neglect research and induction into the tradition in dealing with societal problems. But it must not forget that these are the means for training whole men and not ends in themselves. When knowledge as impersonal product becomes primary, we are on our way to producing Emerson's monsters, distorted fragments of men rather than whole human beings.

108

If the fourth dimension is to be included in college and university education, then personal interchange and ferment are essential. Discussion and disagreement, examining unpopular perspectives as well as the accepted ones, are basic to an education that would train for critical evaluation and balanced judgment. Learning in company with the senior members of the academic community rather than being lectured at by them is necessary if the juniors in the community are to enhance their sense of human concern and moral responsibility. Beyond words there must also be opportunities to take part in responsible decisions and actions. Less mature whole persons must have opportunity for personal contact and involvement with more mature whole persons if the fourth dimension of higher education is to become operative. This may place a strain on educators and public leaders who prefer to relate to their constituencies through lectures, mass media, and organizations. Personal relationships require time and test the moral stamina of the participants.

Perhaps at this point the possibilities of such education become more problematical in the United States. James A. Perkins sees the perils of rigidity in European higher education. The danger exists also in American higher education, and it exists most acutely precisely at this point: the leaders of our colleges and universities, the professors and the administrators have been trained in the specialties of acquiring, transmitting, and applying knowledge and in impersonal modes of relationship, but not in education for responsibility and wholeness. A crisis exists because the need for such education is almost as prevalent among the senior members of our academic community as it is among the junior members.

Possibly, bold and venturesome educators may find ways to enhance the functioning of the dimension of ethical insight and responsibility on their own campuses. We have in the United States a tradition that calls for continued creativity, for experimentation and innovation, for criticism and flexibility. Hopefully, we have not yet become so frozen that this tradition cannot operate to discover new dimensions of higher education and to contribute to the development of whole persons.

3. Meaning and Decision

How does a college develop whole persons rather than Emerson's "walking monsters"? One persuasive answer to this question seems obvious when stated but is very difficult both to understand in deeper than a cerebral fashion and to render operative on most college campuses. Whole persons are developed by placing them in a community where they may interact with older whole persons and their own peers over significant problems of the past, the future, and the present, and where they must make decisions about their own conduct and involvement in society that require ethical reflection and growth in responsibility.

Put this way it sounds incredibly simple and obvious. Furthermore, a college environment approaches perfection as a setting for such a process. Unhappily, the traditional isolation of academic work from real human problems and the long-standing in loco parentis policy of most church-related colleges have made it virtually impossible to contribute greatly toward the development of responsible human beings. At a graduation address several years ago, R. Nevitt Sanford began by remarking that commencements are very sad occasions because they mark the time when students become alumni. When one surveys the results of college training as demonstrated in those who have been subjected to it, there is much basis for pessimism. As increasing numbers of our youth are attending schools and colleges, as the range of technical power and expertise to which students can be exposed has widened, educational processes more and more have isolated students from meaningful contact with educators and with real human problems and have increased the paternalistic control over students, thus preventing the development of responsibility through sharing in important decisions.

Fortunately, powerful forces have been at work to compel changes in college policies and practices. Though resisted by many in positions of authority, changes have taken place in campus practices and in the consciousness of many faculty and students, administrators and trustees, alumni and societal leaders. For one thing, events of the past decade have erased the neat boundaries between campus and society. The Vietnam War, the civil rights struggle, the plight of our cities, the problems of environmental pollution have spilled over onto the campus and the campus has been a prime mover in pressing society to act. For another thing, students have acted to win greater freedom for collegiate young adults. In commenting on the upheaval at Columbia University in 1968, Margaret Mead emphasized that the turmoil there reflected the problems of society

110

and the dissatisfaction of students with their disenfranchised status more than specific grievances about campus structures.[5]

There has been an attempt to isolate education from real living, with its striving for meaning and its irresistible pressure for decision and action. The conviction is stealing over many young adults that living may be more educationally significant than classroom exercises. If the temper of the young seems anti-intellectual, it may be a necessary reaction against the antihumanness of those who pose as intellectuals. This same concern for education filled with significance for human living and relatedness to urgent societal problems is present among many faculty members and reflective administrators as well as in student movements for educational and social reform. It is not "meaning" in some abstract or detached sense that troubles the waters of campus complacency but meaning as it relates to human living and social need. It is meaning as it informs human decision and provides a sense of purpose.

On the part of students, and especially among the sharper ones, there is a strong feeling of having come to the campus for an education and having discovered that the only things available are isolated clumps of specialized information and an examination system based more on regurgitation than appropriation. In the classroom students are subjected to lecture by the wit-and-run method. Their professors appear in fifty-minute epiphanies to provide sixteen prevalent views of any issue without remaining on hand long enough to take a stand on any one of them.

Many students, to be sure, are satisfied to be the recipients of great quantities of information. They have come to college to receive vocational training and want no more than this. They are happy enough with the transmission and regurgitation system because it does not seriously interfere with the extracurricular frolics their departure from the context of parental control now permits. But the students of the sixties let it be known with increasing force that they seek more out of college, and the quieter students of the seventies are no less determined. They seek meaning by which to live, purposes that will give significance to their decisions, and a sense of calling that will make their lives count. It is the better student

---

[5] Margaret Mead, "The Wider Significance of the Columbia Upheaval," in *Columbia Forum*, vol. 11, no. 3, Fall, 1968, pp. 5-6.

who is often most deeply disappointed by the thinness of much that passes for education in colleges. The dropout rate among the best is appalling.

Meaning and decision are intimately interwoven in human living. Ernest Becker writes:

> Man . . . needs a living and daily concern with ultimates, with the mystery of being, and with his role in the perpetuation of being. And rational, technical knowledge . . . cannot give this. . . . The decline of scientific rationalism is no mere "failure of nerve." Rather, it is the stark inadequacy of the scientific quest to the problem of social order and community.[6]

So immured are many professors within their specialized graduate training that all dealing with meaning and purpose, which their best students crave, is avoided deliberately except occasionally when the professor "gets off the subject."

At the height of the Free Speech Movement in Berkeley, Mario Savio, a sharp student by any standards, wrote in criticism of the educational system in the multiversity:

> The university is well structured, well tooled, to turn out people with all the sharp edges worn off, the well-rounded person. . . .
> America is becoming ever more the utopia of sterilized, automated contentment. The "futures" and "careers" for which American students now prepare are for the most part intellectual and moral wastelands. This chrome-plated consumers' paradise would have us grow up to be well-behaved children. But an important minority of men and women coming to the front today have shown that they will die rather than be standardized, replaceable and irrelevant.[7]

When the larger dimensions of education are forgotten and the importance of meaning and decision omitted, then the campus scene and the society around can be bleak and barren indeed where complacent conformity rather than critical insight is inculcated.

Faculty members and administrators, especially the more creative ones, are also disturbed by the reductionist tendencies in collegiate training. They are concerned not only because of what they see

[6] Ernest Becker, *Beyond Alienation: A Philosophy of Education for the Crisis of Democracy.* New York: Braziller, 1967, p. 220.

[7] Mario Savio, "An End to History" in *Humanity,* December, 1964, p. 4.

happening but because of the problems in attempting to go against the flow of events. The explosion of knowledge over the past century has produced a situation in which it appears to be impossible to grapple with the meaning of the whole. Disciplines have multiplied, and specialized areas within each discipline have proliferated. Overall synthesis has moved beyond the range of imagination as the difficulties of achieving competence in one specialized area become harder to deal with. The successes of scholarship based on specialized research ought not to be underestimated, but neither should the dilemmas it poses for meaningful education. As the academic disciplines have divided themselves into smaller and smaller areas of specialization, college courses more and more deal with isolated fragments rather than meaning for man. Ortega y Gassett speaks of the pretentious modern university that is mass producing the "new barbarian," a person better trained than ever before but unable to understand or grapple with the vital system of ideas by which his society lives.

The other side of the explosion of knowledge is the explosion of ignorance. As we advance in specialized knowledge, we know less and less about the whole, about the interrelation of the parts we handle so expertly. We are inundated by information and have lost real sense of direction. The statement of Albert Camus in *The Fall* may describe our situation: "It's not navigating but dreaming." Or perhaps Marshall McLuhan expresses it best in his statement to match the old one about the professor who continues to know more and more about less and less, "The specialist is one who makes no small errors on his way toward the grand fallacy." And so the sense of meaning fades from the central processes of training. A sense of isolation pervades the whole. The arenas of action and decision are elsewhere.

In the present situation return to some system of overarching synthesis is impossible. But we omit the vital center of *higher* education when we cease to wrestle with the problems of meaning. When we attend to the significance of the whole as this relates to human decision, we shall not be on our way toward new absolutes, but we shall be dealing with one of the nagging issues underlying unrest among the students, and we shall be on the path toward discovering new dimensions of the educational process.

4. Toward Renewal

As we have indicated, the quest for new dimensions in higher education is not simply the result of an evolutionary process but has grown with revolutionary rapidity under pressure from activist sections of the student and faculty populace. What is happening may be regarded as no less than the emergence of a new form of higher education, one as different from the research-oriented institution modeled after nineteenth-century German universities as that university differed from its liberal arts predecessor. Any realistic discussion of the church-related college must take place within the context of this larger movement of higher education today.

Though many of the subjects taught in Western education go back as far as the Greek academies, the university as an institution takes its rise in the Middle Ages. In the medieval university, training was centered upon logical discourse and the marshaling of authority in disputation. This was the scholastic university, heavily dependent upon Aristotelian thought and Christian theology.

Out of the Renaissance and Reformation came new interests that found their way into higher education. Renewed interest in the classical period and classical languages, with fresh importance placed upon the Bible and its interpretation, and shifting attention to man and nature led to the development of the college and university centered upon what we call the liberal arts. The focus of this education was to transmit a great tradition stretching back through the centuries and to induct students into membership in the culture this tradition represented. Incredible as it may sound, instruction in Hebrew came into great demand in the sixteenth century because it was a vital tool in the quest for meaning.

Beginning with the founding of the University of Berlin in 1809, another conception of higher education came to the foreground. Here the emphasis was neither on logical disputation nor on transmitting the culture of the past but rather on the advancement of the frontiers of learning. Conceived in this way the university became the place where able scholars gathered to do research and to report the results of their labors in lectures and publications. The frontiers of learning became the focus, not the accumulated wisdom of the past. The research university rapidly came into dominance on the continent, and by the last quarter of the nineteenth century had taken root in the United States. As the graduate schools have risen to dominance in American education and the Ph.D. has become the magic union card licensing one to teach, the liberal arts college has been eclipsed and has become a colony within the graduate empire, furnishing the raw materials of academic ability to be manufactured into finished scholarship in the doctoral factories.[8] Clark Kerr has delineated well the shape of the research university as it has evolved in the United States, calling it at one time the multiversity and at another time the federal grant university.[9]

The excellent descriptions of the American research university that are now being provided may indicate it is already in the afternoon, if not the evening, of its dominance. There are signs all around that a new university is emerging. Professor A. Hunter Dupree of Brown University, commenting on the recurring crises in Berkeley, has said:

> The struggle is not within a single university but rather between two universities in conflict. One, born nearly a century ago and now full of years and success, is the research university that lives in the cubed towers of the modern campus. The other, the existentialist university, has just emerged blinking in the light from the byways of outer society, shouting high aspirations and railing bitterly because it cannot immediately appropriate the property and assets of an institution it considers morally bankrupt.[10]

Certainly the new shape of higher education has existentialist overtones. Several elements must be included. First, there is the demand that education cease pretending to deal with objective bodies of information and attempt to relate the varied spectrum of knowledge into meaning for persons so that the higher learning may be a vehicle for students discovering purpose and calling in life on a deeper level than economic security and material affluence. Second, there is the demand that the academic disciplines overcome their isolation and bring the wealth of multidisciplinary resources to bear on human problems. And third, there is the growing pressure on the university to drop the pretense of ivory-towered research (which actually conceals all too often performing uncritically whatever tasks for which government or industry is willing to provide funds) and

---

[8] See Jencks and Riesman, *The Academic Revolution*, esp. pp. 12-27.
[9] See Clark Kerr, *The Uses of the University*, chapter 2.
[10] A. Hunter Dupree, "Two Universities in Conflict" in *Humanity*, February, 1967, p. 1.

take a more self-conscious and intentional role in the struggle for human rights, in improving society, and in the race against ecological disaster.

The new form of higher education that is now emerging must give up the pretense of neutrality concerning issues of social justice and purpose. It must recognize itself as human in the midst of humanity. The new campus seeks not only to transmit the tradition and research but also to call students to meaningful purpose in their living, to combine educational and social resources to find solutions to urgent human problems, and to enter creatively the marketplace of human need. It strives to become an agent of social change. Some call this new higher education "the existential university." Its more appropriate name is "change-agent university" or "action university." [11]

To explore more carefully what such action requires, we shall focus first on the close and often ill-perceived relationship between governance and education and second on the involvement of colleges in issues of social policy and change. In any event, higher education is taking on increasing responsibility for the shaping of society. It is training persons not merely to be experts but to take responsibility for the welfare of mankind. Education and human aspiration become more closely intertwined than ever before.

If the church-related college is to take part in this movement toward a new higher education, then it must develop programs that relate to the problems and needs of the society around. Whether they are on the fringes of a city or isolated on the plains, colleges must train students to understand and work within the context of urban crisis. Through courses and through time spent abroad students must be prepared to live in a world of colliding cultures. Vietnam and civil rights can no longer be regarded as subjects for extracurricular activities; they must be drawn into the very center of the educational process. Here is one of the most certain clues by means of which the church-related college may find a new identity. It must become a center of planning for its societal constituency and a place where responsible leadership is trained to understand

---

[11] For an excellent and provocative statement on this theme, see James W. White, "The Action University: A New Conceptualization of the Higher Learning." Berkeley: Pacific School of Religion Thesis, 1969.

and seek solutions to the problems that plague mankind. The move out of the ivory tower and into the marketplace will be both threatening and exciting. It will require imagination and vigor not only on the part of administrators but the enlistment of the insights and energies of faculty and students.

Chapter VIII

GOVERNANCE AND EDUCATION

THE POLITICIZATION of higher education began in February, 1960, with the sit-in by black students at a Greensboro lunch counter. The movement spread across the South and then over the entire nation. New dimensions and intensity were given to campus unrest by the Free Speech Movement in Berkeley, 1964. And a crescendo of turmoil wracked the entirety of American higher education in the wake of Richard Nixon's widening of the Indo-China War in the spring of 1970. Since then the tension has diminished, but the campus has not returned to the passivity of the fifties. What is the meaning of this overt politicization of higher education? What are its implications for the educational process? Some of its clearest meaning, I am convinced, concerns the relation of governance to education.

Controversy is not new to the American campus. Tension has always existed between "town and gown." Two aspects of the situation that developed in the sixties seem especially significant: the character of the turmoil on campus became national with reference both to the movement and the issues of unrest; and the tension on campus was part of a crisis involving our entire society. Based in part upon detailed coverage by the mass communication media and in part upon the issues involved, the tension that emerged in the sixties is national rather than local. Ecology, the Indo-Chinese War, urban disorder, and minority rights are issues for the entire society, not for colleges and universities alone. Governance in higher education today concerns not only campus matters but societal policies and interests as well. And conversely the public is intensely concerned about what happens on campus because higher education is a prime national resource and the interests served by education are vital to the nation as a whole as well as to specific groups within it. Campus unrest is national because higher education plays an influential role in shaping the future of our society and world.

Because the campus is more important than ever before, it is not surprising that the conflict in and around higher education has intensified. Demonstrations occur, the police and the national guard are called in, people are killed and property damaged because much is at stake. We would not be exaggerating to say that we are passing through the most serious crisis in our national life since the Civil War and higher education is, for good reason, at the center of the struggle. The battles for educational reform and for Black Studies Programs, over research policies and the Asian debacle, concerning the environment and the quality of urban life are not merely over college rules and procedures but about the purposes, policies, and cherished values of the nation. The intensity has increased because it is a political struggle of societal proportions with the future as the stake.

Only in political terms can we understand what is happening in higher education and grasp the intimate interrelationship of campus and society. A new identity for the church-related college in its public present is not possible without awareness of the political dimensions of education and the educational significance of political processes.

1. The Politics of Higher Education

The leadership of a college or university always has been a political task in relation to trustees, alumni, faculty, students, other constituencies, and society at large. Today it is clearly as public a political post as that of any local, state, or federal official. The wise saying of Harry Truman applies equally, "If you can't stand the heat, stay out of the kitchen."

Many persons question the propriety of discussing the politics of higher education just as they also resist talking about politics in the churches. One can find academicians willing, at the drop of a footnote, to discuss politics in Saigon, Sacramento, or Washington, but who regard discussion of power relations in their own colleges as

119

embarrassing. If politics deals with the way a community makes decisions, if politics has to do with power and its exercise, if politics concerns who gets what, when, where, and how, then obviously there is a politics of higher education, and we must understand it better if we are to contend with the realities of campus events.

The political dimensions of the interaction among campus groups and of the interrelations of campus and society now seem obvious to most observers. But this has not always been so. Perhaps because it has been considered in bad taste or perhaps through some strange bit of inadvertence, little has been written on the politics of higher education. John D. Millett, himself a political scientist, in explaining the challenge that led to his book on organization in higher education, says: "I had to admit that political science as a discipline had given slight attention to higher education as an activity of the state. There was little in the writing on government in this country to illuminate the operation of our colleges and universities." [1] Nor have commentators on higher education until recently made much use of political analysis in their writings. Three books with the same title illustrate this circumstance. Thorstein Veblen,[2] who saw with singular and cynical clarity the context of social forces within which higher education existed, emphasized factors related to economics and social status rather than to politics. Robert M. Hutchins,[3] writing in the thirties, deplores the demonic effects of the love of money, a misconception of democracy, an erroneous notion of progress, etc., on colleges and universities, presents a caustic description of educational confusion, and proposes a plan to distinguish general education from what is appropriate to a university. But attention to the political processes necessary to the higher learning, a matter about which Hutchins knows much, is notably lacking. Knowledge in Hutchins' treatment does not include knowing *how*, a most unplatonic and unpolitical state of affairs. By the time Paul Woodring[4] wrote in the 1960s, the spectrum of issues considered appropriate to

---

[1] John D. Millett, *The Academic Community: An Essay on Organization.* New York: McGraw-Hill, 1962, p. vii.

[2] Thorstein Veblen, *The Higher Learning in America.* New York, 1935. Veblen's work was published in 1918.

[3] Robert M. Hutchins, *The Higher Learning in America.* New Haven: Yale University Press, 1936.

[4] Paul Woodring, *The Higher Learning in America: A Reassessment.* New York: McGraw-Hill, 1968.

a discussion of higher education had broadened considerably. Prestige and sex, as well as the wide-ranging studies of students, are given fleeting attention. Woodring recognizes that the demarcations between campus and society are no longer as precise as in the past. And the political implications of education have become too apparent not to creep into the discussion. But he almost succeeds in ignoring the subject by stressing the familiar themes of diversity, growth, money, and cutting the educational pie. The one section that promises a treatment of politics proves to be a cursory and superficial discussion of "the power structure of academic institutions," ending with the suggestion that students be allowed to rate the faculty and recommend curricular changes. The campus is reduced to narrowly academic concerns, and the deeper political issues emerging today are ignored. By contrast, educators over the past decade have been forced to give attention to politics, to the relation between education and politics, and to the interpenetration of campus and societal issues. As a result, the publication of books and articles on campus governance is increasing with greater attention to political dimensions.[5]

Church-related colleges might have hoped for help in understanding the politics of higher education from the field of social ethics in theological seminaries. Unhappily, as this new area of study developed, it gave attention to politics, economics, sociology, and international relations, but omitted education. As a result, neither the place of colleges and universities in the political economy nor political, economic, and sociological understanding of higher education were included. Religion in higher education developed apart from social ethics as a field devoted to training seminarians for "student work" or the advocacy of curricular religion, not, as would have been more appropriate, as an area of social ethics.

To provide an introductory view of the politics of higher education, let us look at some sources of political difficulties confronting colleges and universities.

---

[5] See especially Harold L. Hodgkinson and L. Richard Meeth (eds.), *Power and Authority: Transformation of Campus Governance*. San Francisco: Jossey-Bass, 1971. Older books, perceptive and helpful though rendered in part obsolete by events of the sixties, are John J. Corson, *Governance of Colleges and Universities*, New York: McGraw-Hill, 1960, and John D. Millett, *The Academic Community*.

The sheer growth of higher education means that it occupies a place of high visibility and power in American society. The number of students enrolled in 1900 was slightly over two hundred thousand. We shall soon have nine million. Projections for the next decades suggest that the number will increase. The budget for higher education nationally must be stated in the billions. Faculty members are making up a sizable and influential proportion of our population. The college and university, in terms of the dollars they disburse and the personnel they involve, exert great power in our national life.

It is especially the students who have brought the political problems of higher education to the fore. Rather than fitting neatly our stereotyped image of the eager high school graduate venturing off to the big university to discover a wider world, today's student is older than his counterpart of fifty years ago. He is continuing his education into professional and graduate schools. He is vastly more experienced because he was reared on TV, travels more widely, and involves himself more often in social issues—in antiwar demonstrations, in urban ghetto work, in Mississippi marches, and service projects around the world. This older, more experienced student finds himself in conflict with the political patterns on campus held over from a time when college exercised parental care and authority. He is dissatisfied, and he makes his dissatisfaction known!

If the new student, through his protests and social activism, has made the political problems of higher education visible, then the widened functions of higher education have provided virtually every sector of our society with a political stake in the campus. Increasing need for money from state legislatures, the federal government, and private donors keeps the college and university at the center of public attention. But the reason that higher education has been able to command so much of the nation's wealth is that the university is now indispensable for the functioning of the nation. The campus is politically powerful because it trains much of the personnel to operate the social system, because it produces new knowledge and new techniques by which society can function better, and because it provides new sources of power without which the nation cannot maintain its place in the modern world. Higher education is a prime national resource. What happens on campus is of crucial importance to all those who are concerned about the welfare of the country. By the functions it has come to perform the university wields great political power and therefore is a center of political storm.[6] John Kenneth Galbraith is undoubtedly correct when he says the university has become so important to industry and to the government that it is beyond danger of being destroyed or its operation seriously impaired. But for the same reason it is caught up in the maelstrom of contending political forces with many interests seeking to control it.

Still another source of difficulty can now be seen. Why can the students make themselves felt as a political force within the university and within society? It is partly a matter of their large numbers, but not completely. The more important reason is that *society needs the talents of the students* as never before. In spite of the new thousands flooding onto the campus every fall, the demand for trained personnel has grown rapidly since World War II. The student, except for the period of the Nixon depression, has been finding himself in a seller's market, with churches and social agencies, industry and government, professional and graduate schools competing for his energies. These older, more numerous, more experienced students recognize the need society has for them and are making demands in return or dropping out. The situation gives them political power, and they are organizing to use it.

These are the major sources of the political difficulties surrounding the campus. They can no longer be ignored. We must think and act in terms of the politics of higher education.

Now let us look at the central political problems. Foremost among them is the inadequacy of the political processes within the campus and those governing the interaction between the college and society. Patterns of decision-making still in use were developed in an era when higher education was smaller, had far more simple relationships to society, and dealt with fewer, younger, less-mature students. The rapid changes that have been taking place in the university, society, and the student body have left these old political patterns completely outmoded. Events of the past two decades as higher education has grown and become increasingly complex have repeatedly raised the question whether the present trustee-regent sys-

---

[6] Harold L. Hodgkinson, "A Look Ahead," in *Power and Authority*, writes: "Ironically, the fact that campuses are now being torn asunder is due in part to their success, and to their importance in American life" (p. 208).

tem of control is adequate. A recent study of an eastern church-related university disclosed its trustees to have an average age in excess of seventy and to be composed of over half clergymen, despite the stated aim to develop the university in new and public directions.

Can controlling bodies remote from students and faculty, unaware of new functions and purposes, meet the demands placed upon colleges and universities today? Can the present pattern of governance cope with the diversity that comprises the scene of higher education? If plans made now about courses, student participation, and the involvement of the college with societal needs are subject to arbitrary veto, then no educational process that is innovative can be undertaken, and change both within the college and in its relation to society cannot take place without confrontation and upheaval.

The present pattern of governance derives from an era when autocratic procedures in government and business as well as on campus were accepted. Politics has been greatly democratized in American society, but too little democratization has occurred in colleges and universities. Campus political procedures do not provide an adequate role for students and often leave faculty participation in a highly uncertain status.

When the close relation existing between college and society is taken into account, the politics of higher education emerges with even greater clarity. Traditionally, colleges in this country have served as a finishing school for children of the upper social groups and to transmit the major elements of Western culture to those who would occupy positions of leadership in American society. The technical and research university developed to expand human knowledge and manipulative power and places these advances in the service of industrial and governmental goals. A new movement in higher education, appearing occasionally earlier, would harness the innovative energies of higher education to purposes of social change and the realization of a more human world.

The old liberal arts college is the prime example of the first type. It was dominant in the era when higher education was primarily for the wealthy classes and for especially promising persons from lower socioeconomic groups. The affluent supported colleges financially, sat on college boards, were dominant in their administrative positions, supplied many of their professors, and expected their offspring

124

to acquire in college the cultural background and social skills that would stamp them as members of the ruling class. In spite of the vast growth and changes that have taken place in higher education over the past century, the most prestigious and best-financed colleges still serve this function for higher socioeconomic groups. Growing affluence and the forces of democratization have altered the pattern but not the fact. These upper strata of American society have a long-standing and powerful interest in our colleges and universities. In this century, higher education has become the focus of an intense political struggle between those who wish to protect significant sectors of the system from invasion by the masses and those who wish to make all higher education available on an equal basis to all citizens. One need only examine data reporting where the federal cabinet officers and board members of the larger financial institutions went to college in order to recognize the intimate relation existing between higher education and the political-economic power of the nation.

The development and nature of the technical-research university and its counterpart activities in colleges provide another clue to the close ties between higher education and political processes in society. Money for agricultural, industrial, and military research has increased steadily over the past century and has reached astronomical proportions since World War II. Clark Kerr refers to the institutions that are the greatest beneficiaries of governmental research funds as federal grant universities. But this side of history omits the even larger amounts spent in facilities operated by industry and government that depend on the expertise of those trained in higher education and on the staffs of colleges and universities. Radical students in the sixties found ample evidence on the public record to support the charge that institutions and scholars were prostituting themselves to the exploitative and imperialist purposes of big business and big government. Whether one joins the protests against these "uses of the university" or considers them valid, the location of higher education at the center of political conflict is clear.

The emergence of movements advocating educational reform and seeking to make colleges and universities agents of humane social change has only enlarged the dimensions and intensity of the political character of the campus. The central purposes of society and the allocation of national priorities are as certainly at stake in the struggle over educational process as in the political maneuvering in Washington and in state capitals over public budgets.

When the relationship between higher education and conflicting societal interests is lifted into view, the political character of the campus becomes obvious. It is equally clear that the political processes within colleges and universities and between higher education and societal constituencies are not adequate to contain the struggles now in process. Student governments of the past have been equipped to deal only with "sandbox" issues. Faculty organization has not been especially adequate even for academic affairs much less for resolving the complex issues concerning the relations of education to societal goals and functions. The trustee system, moderately viable for an earlier era, finds board members caught between their own busy lives and the increasing demands of recurring crises, between a policy of authority delegated to president and faculty and the temptation to meddle in the details of academic life about which they know little, between the pressures of powerful political interests and the rising tide of campus protest, between the tradition of academic freedom and the expectation that higher education should provide any service requested. A crucial problem today revolves around older, outmoded patterns of authority and the effort to develop new ones fast enough to cope with changing conditions on campus and in society.[7]

2. The Meaning of Governance

Whether recognized or not, education and politics are closely related. The educational process includes, if learning is to be significant, the entire pattern of community, the fabric of relationships, and especially the modes of governance. Along with other facets, politics involves the way a community makes its decisions, and decisions imply taking responsibility for the choice made. Education is acquiring information, but even more it is learning how to use information, becoming more mature in taking responsibility for the decisions of one's own life, and understanding the way in which

---

[7] For an illuminating treatment of the themes treated in this chapter, with lessons drawn from the troubled scene of Berkeley and suggestions for new patterns of governance in the University of California, see Caleb Foote, Henry Mayer, and Associates, *The Culture of the University: Governance and Education.* San Francisco: Jossey-Bass, 1969.

those decisions involve the lives and well-being of the community to which one belongs. In this sense the political dimensions of education take shape and provide the basis of harsh judgment on the shoddy performance of many colleges in training for responsibility.

In this perspective the patterns of governance of the college community are integrally important for the education that takes place there rather than as apart from and transcending the context of learning. The style of governance on campus in combination with the style of the home from which they come may do more to shape the response of students to persons in the community around them than courses from respected scholars in political science or the humanities. Writing about the beginnings of the Free Speech Movement at Berkeley immediately after the events, Richard L. Gelwick said: "What kind of politics universities foster was vividly illustrated recently at the University of California, and higher education looked feeble as a teacher of American political process." And he concluded: "As we go through a national campaign that once again reveals the American weakness for personality politics, for ignoring policy and issues, and the moral smear, we ought to question what the practice of politics on campus has contributed to this phenomenon." [8]

Patterns of governance within colleges and universities cannot be borrowed from business and public administration. John J. Corson points out that colleges and universities have "different functions requiring a different organization and different practices than are common in business or governmental enterprises." [9] John D. Millett goes further and suggests that patterns borrowed from industry and government may subvert the educative process.

Excessive emphasis on administrative efficiency and fiscal stability may go far toward distorting educational goals. An exciting campus may require a wider spectrum of ideas present than wealthy donors would approve. A tight bureaucracy may dampen or even extinguish the exciting play of experiment and invention among students and faculty. On today's campus, the general absence of political processes by means of which persons may have a share in decisions affecting

---

[8] Richard L. Gelwick, "Education in Political Practice," in *Humanity*, November, 1964, pp. 4-5.

[9] John J. Corson, *Governance of Colleges and Universities*, p. 5.

their lives means frustration and alienation for many. It is often difficult to discover ways in which authority is exercised and decisions made. That is not only bad politics; it is also bad education.

In a far more complex sense, however, college governance may be at the root of the problem of meaning. As higher education has grown, it has produced organization and departmentalized function. Chasms have developed between different sectors of the campus. What appears routine procedure to a registrar may appear as arbitrary "nitpicking" to the student. There is less sense of working together in a single community than was present when the campus was smaller, less awareness of sharing common purposes and loyalties. We often say that higher education has become depersonalized or that there is a breakdown in communication.

When students speak of depersonalization on the campus they are certainly not asking for more chumminess with the president and the faculty. And they certainly are not asking for greater paternalistic control of their lives. Instead, they are asking to be respected as persons and are requesting a responsible role in the decisions that shape their education and by which they are expected to live on campus.

Alienation of persons from the community in which they live derives not from a sense of conflicting purposes and interests so much as from being excluded from the processes of governance. In the old societies governed by royalty, alienation was often overcome by a sense of identification with the ruler and the conviction that he acted in behalf of his people. The monarch who despised or lost this identity risked revolution or assassination. In the old liberal arts college, loyalty to alma mater and participation in her rites provided a sense of identity. In a democratic society and in higher education as it has become increasingly democratized, a sense of identity is achieved and alienation is overcome by taking part in community decisions. To the extent that college administrators have not learned these lessons from the political order, they risk revolution and career assassination, as some of them have discovered to their distress.

More is involved, however, than overcoming alienation. Education is the central purpose of a college community. In line with this goal it is necessary to seek for and change toward an educational model of governance. Ways must be found to use the entire community in the process of learning rather than classroom lectures and laboratory experiment alone. Critical reflection and responsible action cannot be instilled merely by golden rhetoric from distinguished presidents and successful trustees while the students, who we hope are learning to think and act responsibly, are denied any part in community processes. Marshall McLuhan's statement that "the medium is the message" applies with special force to education. Transposed to the campus, McLuhan's insight means that the entire shape of the college community will be the message communicated and the education projected. The pattern of governance as medium is the educational message of the college, a disturbing thought indeed when one considers the petty tyrannies operative from presidential offices and the departmental baronies on many a college campus. It is in this light that it becomes essential to examine the pattern of governance within the academic community and the ways in which it serves or subverts the education intended.

3. The Function of Community

We are suggesting that education takes place not only in classrooms, laboratories, and residence halls but also in the entire college community, and we mean more than that education takes place in many particular places. The whole campus educates for good or ill. Indeed it may be the most encompassing and important dimensions of learning that take place not in this or that place but in the encounter with the whole.

Church-related colleges are concerned about Christian education. In line with this interest, classes in the Bible, world religions, theology, and ethics are provided. Chapel services, either compulsory or voluntary, are conducted. Certainly classes in religion are an appropriate part of any curriculum that intends to deal comprehensively with our cultural heritage. And worship may play an important role in aiding persons in their attempts to cope with problems of identity and vocation. There is much doubt, however, that religion can be taught by conventional classroom methods. Education in faith, in those commitments by which we decide and act in our moments of responsibility, cannot be learned from textbooks or lectures or even sermons, though this is not to say that each of these does not have a place in academic and worshiping communities. Education in faith takes place in the relationships, the interaction, and the dimensions of one's total situation. It is crucial, therefore, that those who take responsibility for the conduct of church-related colleges heed the fabric of human community.

Man is a communal being. As human beings, we emerge as persons within a pattern of relationships, relationships defined in part by our natural organic context but more centrally in their human dimensions defined by communal interpersonal relations. In the view of John Macmurray there is no such thing as an individual; there is never one person until there are two.[10] In terms of our own experience there is never one person until there is a community of persons. These relationships are not empty but laden with meaning. We become persons through responding to persons. Who we are is made up of this pattern of response within a communal context. More than response, however, there is responsibility, accountability, present in the relations of our living. We are able to respond, and we feel intensely the burden of the consequences of our actions.

The communal relationships of "personhood" are also a context of commitments. The community through which we become aware of ourselves as persons contains the commitment of persons to one another and to common language, understanding, and purposes. We enter into personhood as we come to participate in these commitments. We commit ourselves to the language system and come to dwell in a culture. We commit ourselves to persons and become part of a family and community. We commit ourselves to purposes and become part of the action of society. On the most intensely personal level we are defined by our loyalties and disloyalties, that is, by those persons and causes to which we are faithful and by our unfaithfulness. We share in certain communities because we share their loyalty to a common goal, and we are outside other communities because we reject the causes for which those communities live.

Our actions in relationship, understood as laden with these meanings, constitute the primary fabric of our lives. Our understanding of ourselves, our neighbor, the world, and the sovereign reality of that world is defined by our community and takes on meaning for us within it. Reflective knowledge and criticism operate within a context given us by our social matrix. When man is viewed in this way it becomes clear that the most important learning of his life takes

---

[10] See John Macmurray, *The Self as Agent*. London: Faber & Faber, Limited, 1957. See also *Persons in Relation*. New York: Harper, 1961.

place not in the presentation of sheer information but in the context of relationship. It has been shown that children who have no relationships in which they are loved and accepted can scarcely control motor activity, much less learn the skills of language and the lessons of the schoolroom. This is true on an unacknowledged level for all of us. It is probable that no one learns apart from meaningful relation.

Though this view of learning holds also for administration and faculty, it has its clearest application to students. College-age youth may be seen most adequately not as student but as young adult. Now isolated in considerable measure from the relationships of home and local community, the young adult on campus forms new communities and other meaningful relations through which to understand himself and by which to guide his life. The importance of peer groups for the young adult has long been recognized. The relationship to those of his own age exercises great control over the life and learning of the young adult because here he finds friendship and acceptance. But college learning must not be left within the peer group. The relationships of the young adult to older nonparental adults are essential if his learning is to take place within the wider horizons offered by professor, classroom, and library. For meaningful relations to be present that will open these wider horizons, the young adult has need for "guarantors," the nonparental adults who will relate to him with friendship and share with him in openness their vision and their values. Such a context of meaningful relations on campus is not peripheral to the academic experience but constitutes its center.

In these ways the fabric of relation and pattern of governance within the campus community are essential for education. Responsibility to the young adult on campus is not fulfilled by providing a vast array of information apart from the context of relationships and opportunities for exercising responsibility that will open him to learning.

As colleges have grown larger and the scholar's life more specialized, the fabric of community has often become frayed or even allowed to fall apart. Relationships are ignored or destroyed as the faculty becomes preoccupied with professional advancement and research for publication and as administrators become preoccupied with prestige, financial development, and a campus community free

131

of disturbances that might create unpleasant publicity. At the time in his life when the young adult is most hungry for new relationships that will take him into the cultural heritage and provide him with a significant vocation, he often finds himself excluded from all meaningful community except that of his peers. If the authentically religious dimensions of education take place in the holistic pattern, then the shape of the educational community—its forms of governance and relation—takes on more importance than the parts seen in isolation. When one considers how little attention is given to community conceived in these terms, it is scarcely surprising that we are disappointed with the results of our fragmented efforts to teach religion.

In the community of personal relationship that is provided in home and local community, it is altogether likely that persons can believe the ultimate reality of the world is also personal and concerned with them. When the student steps onto the campus and finds himself confronted with impersonal bureaucracy, computerized registration procedures, and machine examinations, it is not surprising to find him dropping his belief in a personal deity and adopting a view of ultimate reality consonant with the fabric of the community that confronts him. Developing a community that supports significant learning becomes a critical task of higher education today and one that church-related colleges must be sensitive to if they are to discover a viable new identity. When one considers the importance of the fabric of community, the relationship of governance and education emerges as central in the learning process.

4. Education by Involvement

"Community of authority" is the phrase John Millett uses to describe an educational model of governance in higher education. Many educators have doubts that authority can be shared with students. Conditioned by the patterns of governance in business and public administration, where efficiency of production and coherent policy are primary goals, most administrators and faculty tend toward the view that a community of authority would not only lead to chaos but also are convinced that it is an impossible operational mode. The position I propose here, and one coming to increasing acceptance among perceptive educators, is that no pattern of governance other than a community of authority can produce the educational process essential to American society.[11] Undoubtedly no formulation of communally shared authority can produce either the efficiency of operation or the coherence of policy possible within a hierarchical, centralized order. But efficiency and organizational coherence are at best secondary purposes for a college or university, and education with humane breadth and critical depth is a primary purpose. College administrators often centralize authority with the notion that this will please business leaders and public figures among the trustees and wealthy donors. The result quite often is, on the one hand, that the societal leaders are not given an education in the purposes of the college they wish to serve, and, on the other hand, that the more perceptive among these leaders have broader educational vision than the academic administrators with whom they work. Whether or not it can be attained easily, it seems increasingly clear that the development of a community of authority is necessary on all campuses if the purposes of education are to be fulfilled.

Within a pattern of governance based on community of authority, the entire campus is seen as the arena of education. In the first place, ferment is regarded as essential in allowing multiple viewpoints to be presented, unpopular as well as popular ones. Perspectives that the interests of students lead them toward must be explored as well as the "more balanced" ones of professors. But the diversity to be cultivated must be more than intellectual. It must be woven into the entire fabric of decision-making in the college community. Alternative views among faculty and students on intellectual matters will be productive educationally, but so also will be disagreement over curriculum and campus discipline. Inclusion of students in working through matters of policy and procedure for the entire college will prove to be an important vehicle of education. Indeed it may be the area in which the intellectual issues will be tried out and rendered operative in the lives of students.

Here, I believe, is the key to training in overall moral responsibility, in utilizing knowledge rather than merely memorizing it, in integrating information into the process of deciding and acting with

---

[11] For some of the changes under way in governing bodies, see *College and University Trustees*, Educational Testing Service, 1968; Ray Muston, "Governance Changes Are Catching Colleges by Surprise," *College and University Business*, July, 1969; and Hodgkinson and Meeth (eds.), *Power and Authority: Transformation of Campus Governance*, San Francisco: Jossey-Bass, 1971.

moral purpose. The process will be scarcely as efficient as that of centralized authority. Policies will never be completely clear as long as the more immature perspectives of students are included, but the involvement of the entire academic community in working through sensitive areas of policy and regulation will evoke a kind of commitment not possible on most contemporary campuses. Hard decisions about academic freedom and the pressures of society will be faced by students as well as by anxiety-ridden presidents, and the compromises made will provide the circumstance of an education in politics no classroom could offer. Why should students, faculty, or trustees be shielded from the ambiguities of policy? Student governments most often have no real authority, and the students call them sandbox or Mickey Mouse. Our classroom education, carefully isolated from the difficult decisions of the college community, would usually be sandbox too were it not for the rewards and punishment provided in the grade system. It is not efficient use of student energies to isolate education from reality when the wealth of educational opportunities is present in the processes of shaping social policy for the college community.

To make actual a community of authority it is necessary that all sectors and levels of the campus be represented where crucial issues are raised and central decisions made. Trustees usually operate at a distance, a distance carefully promoted by many presidents. The administration operates in geographical proximity but organizational distance from the students and quite often from the faculty. Faculty decisions are made as though the wisdom of the world can come to fruition only when professors meet behind closed doors. Students not only find themselves excluded from the process of decision-making that governs their lives but find it necessary most often to engage in mass demonstrations or sit-ins to assure that their viewpoints will even be noted. The alumni are regarded as a reservoir of funds on which to pour unctuous oil should the reservoir become troubled. Interaction among these isolated groups might prove enlightening for all. Each Harvard overseer, for example, takes time to participate in some of the university's operation. He has the benefit of association with professors and students and they with him. As a result, they learn from one another much that is useful in their respective tasks related to the university.

Participation of students and faculty should begin as soon as the

134

freshman or the new instructor steps onto the campus. He not only deserves to know but will become a more responsible member of the community if he is instructed in the traditions of the college, its patterns of operation, its financial structure, its tenure system, the problems it faces, the pressures upon it, and its plans for the future. For the sake of his loyalty as well as the utilization of his insights, every faculty member, whether junior or senior, should participate on some administrative committee and be aware of the operation of them all, including such things as committees on business procedures, money raising, student recruitment, athletics, and development, as well as academic affairs. After a brief period of induction into the college community, students should be placed in larger self-regulating communities in which administrators share but do not control. The longer a student is on campus, the wider should be the sphere of responsibility he takes for his life and education. By the time a student is a junior or senior the primary communities in which he participates within the college should have representatives on the central governing bodies and committees. We have seen student abilities exercised in civil rights and demonstrations for educational reform. It might occur to enlightened administrators to enlist these energies on behalf of the college.

One may call this dreaming, but similar sounds of deprecation have been made by aristocrats in the face of every possible extension of democratic process. To be included in the pattern of governance will overcome much of the alienation present among college students in relation to the college administration and curriculum. More important, however, it will provide an arena as important as the classroom for education through involvement and responsibility. I have watched on many levels the fascinating attempts of paternalistic faculty and administrations to keep students in a protracted infancy. At the high school level it is said that students are too ignorant and immature to take control of their lives, and much evidence can be produced to support this point of view. But one also hears college administrators and professors saying the same thing: college students are too ignorant and immature to take responsibility for their own lives. And in some measure it is undoubtedly still true. When on the professional and graduate level, however, one hears the same thing from professors and presidents, one begins to suspect that it is they who are too ignorant and immature to share authority rather

135

than the students in their late twenties, many married and with children and taking junior professional responsibilities, who are unable to contribute substantially to the decisions shaping the curriculum in which they are trained and the regulations governing their lives as students. These "immature" students, certainly on the college level and in many cases on the high school level, are taking on impressive responsibilities in many spheres of community life and carrying them out well. The student who has led civil rights demonstrations or taken major responsibility in operating summer camps, or traveled around the world, can scarcely be expected to remain placid when he is asked to return to the sandbox in the fall.

A community of authority does not necessarily mean that all authority is turned over to the junior members of the community or even that the one-man, one-vote applies in an academic society. But it does mean that every member of the community takes part in the process, is represented where important decisions are made, and is called to discover his education occurring throughout the entire fabric of his college experience.

Not in the conventional sense of instruction in religion, but in a more profound way, a model of governance based upon a community of authority is genuinely theological education. When one is called to make decisions bearing on the total life of his community, then one must bring the entire resources of his life to bear. This is what responsibility means and requires of us. When we are uninvolved, it is not really education, except on the edges of living and learning. When we invest our total selves, then we find ourselves confronted by God.

This statement may seem to presuppose a peculiar concept of God. I doubt that this is the case unless we have lost touch with our biblical roots and seek for God in particular places as we look for a box or a chair. Gilbert Ryle tells the story of the man who wanted to see the university and complained that he found only classrooms, libraries, and laboratories. It was necessary to tell him that one does not have classrooms, libraries, laboratories *and* the university, but rather classrooms, libraries, and laboratories *of* the university. As the word university means the encompassing relationship giving reality to the visible parts of a campus, so also in the biblical heritage our God means the encompassing commitments of our life that bind the parts into a whole and on whom we rely as the sovereign power of reality. Theological education therefore takes place in the deepest meaning, not in the sandbox, but when a community of authority calls forth and compels the involvement of total selves in decision and responsible action.

The politics of democracy has revolutionized Western society. Now winds of change are blowing on campus. We must move toward greater democracy in the politics of college and university, not because of pressure from students, but because better politics means better education and, as a result, more capable and morally responsible leadership in all sectors of society.

Chapter IX

THE COLLEGE AND SOCIAL CHANGE

WHEN GOD decided to create the world, it is reliably reported, the conservative angels appeared before him with tears in their eyes and shouted, "O Lord, do not destroy chaos." This original opposition to change is the predecessor of all the subsequent attempts to preserve the status quo that have occurred whenever the slightest alteration in procedure or purpose has been proposed. The present clearly is no exception. But change is occurring today more rapidly than ever before in virtually every sector of society. Educational institutions, which ought to be preparing students and societal leaders for the future, more often than not are so oriented toward the past that they are not even preparing their students for the present. The church-related college at least as much as any other activity in American society must be willing to consider wide-ranging innovation, even knowing that many conservative "angels" will oppose any shift in educational process or campus governance.

No change is more needed today than for higher education to discard the pretense of neutrality on important social issues and to participate selectively and self-consciously in the societal process in which all educational institutions are immersed. Such a shift will not be easy for many colleges and universities, for they have attempted to preserve a dubious and precarious immunity to political and economic pressures by claims to academic freedom based on isolation and nonpartisanship in regard to controversial issues. However difficult the transition, the shift toward overt societal involvement will not only make for greater honesty but will in most instances aid in resolving the identity crisis of the college. It is precisely the pretense of noninvolvement that creates a "credibility gap" between administration and socially aware constituencies, especially students, on the one hand, and between college and conservative constituencies on the other, and deepens the institutional identity crisis.

Higher education in America has probably never been as isolated in an ivory tower as the romantics and superrealists often suppose. Colleges have served the upper social strata by inducting the young into the heritage of the elite groups and affirming their values. Universities have served the institutional church and civil government, agriculture and industry, the military and the space program. Conscientious qualms about serving the purposes of social groups seem most often to emerge when the groups served happen to be the oppressed and the powerless. To many, assertions about academic neutrality appear to be sheer hypocrisy, a pretense to conceal the close relation between higher education and established interests. The issue is no longer whether to remain in an illusory ivory tower but rather what movements to relate to and in what ways.

If neutrality is not an option, then colleges must become aware of the social groups to which they are already related and through these relationships take responsibility to examine critically and participate in reshaping the social policies that are informing society at various levels, determining actions taken by social groups, and contributing to the greater or lesser humanness of man's environment. This will require considerable change in many stated goals of education, greater ethical sensitivity and appreciation of dissent, discovery of ways to educate for social change, and a curricular style that combines commitment, expertise, and leadership.

Increasingly, colleges are discovering that *excellence*, that educational slogan once so safe and sane, is not enough. What kind of excellence and for what purposes must be explored. Education of the Harvard-Stanford variety may not exemplify the kind of excellence appropriate for Iowa Wesleyan or Bishop College. Education has social purposes built into it that must be chosen and affirmed rather than ignored or stated erroneously.

One clear directive for colleges today is that they educate for social change rather than for social stasis. This does not mean the abolition of history or an intentional ignoring of the past in favor of exclusive involvement with the immediately present. Much energy devoted to change fumbles opportunities because of inadequate understanding of what led to the present situation and what comparable precedents may prove illuminating. But the past studied for the purpose of informing action for change now is a quite different sort of history from that studied to confirm the status quo or for strictly antiquarian interests. Social change involves minimally appreciation of the past and projection of alternative futures. But it also requires willingness to launch out, to seek a newer world, to join man's age-old quest into the unknown.

Involvement with social change includes also appreciation of the function of dissent and protest in the opening up of new possibilities for the future. In the sixties, educators, elected officials, and much of the public at large have been opposed to any form of protest. Though protest can be destructive, just as also can excessive attachment to tradition, dissent serves important functions in disclosing the inadequacies and injustices of present forms, in developing new structures of power, and in providing social space for change and innovation.

The most difficult task of all for colleges that take social policy and change seriously is finding an educational style that develops in students, faculty, and participants from various constituencies the ability to combine commitment, expertise, and leadership on significant levels of community involvement. We shall make some suggestions toward such education.

Church-related colleges have a special responsibility to regard the churches, considered both as institution and as movements of Christian faith, as constituencies to be related to their total education process. The churches and society at large, as well as the colleges themselves, will suffer if this responsibility is neglected.

1. Excellence for What?

If it can be nailed down to a specific time, then it was in 1957 after the Russians launched *sputnik* into an orbit in space that excellence became the universal slogan for American education. To be sure, it had never been totally absent. But supplying leaders for church and state or providing persons trained in socially useful skills or giving everyone equal access to the benefits of education— these purposes had seemed to predominate at various periods in the

American past. After 1957, it was excellence. The Russian achievement shocked American governmental leaders, captains of industry, and educators in all fields, especially in the physical sciences. Even the man in the street seemed alarmed by the instruments in the hands of our enemies. Many were ready to push the panic button and dash off in all directions.

Criticism of American education for its softness toward mediocrity and its alleged lack of content became standard. Books on the plight of the schools and what ought to be done became best sellers. A call to excellence was heard throughout the land. Schools, colleges, and universities heeded the change in public sentiment and shifted stated goals.

In retrospect, we can see that much of the criticism was indeed accurate. All too many schools and colleges met the rising tide of students in the wake of World War II by reducing standards to an unhappily low common denominator. Bright students were left unchallenged and bored. The wave of concern did much to improve and diversify education. But there were also some less desirable results. For example, the sudden and excessive emphasis on mathematics and the sciences that tended to stifle interest in social science, the humanities, and the arts. Happily, countervailing forces emerged to this overemphasis. Fists on the panic button gradually relaxed.

For one thing, a comparison of Russian and American education disclosed fewer differences in regard to mathematics and the sciences than was at first supposed. For another, *sputnik* was seen to be the result of a policy of intensive effort and commitment of massive national resources to rocket propulsion rather than the superiority of Russian education. Policies of the administration in Washington, surrounded by a haze of nuclear complacency and the rhetoric of massive retaliation, had directed resources elsewhere. When the White House and the Pentagon changed policy, personnel with appropriate education and skills were found to put objects and persons into space with amazing speed.

Educators, meantime, had been hypnotized by the call to excellence and found themselves left with the question: excellence for what? The uncertain answers to that query, the mindless pressure placed upon students in the wake of *sputnik*, and the rising tide of concern over civil rights and, later, over an immoral and stupid war in Southeast Asia created much of the turmoil on campus and in society at large in the decade of the sixties.

Excellence does not exist in an educational vacuum unrelated to goals and methods, anymore than a call to be pragmatic has any significance apart from ends to be achieved and criteria for what can be said to work in achieving those ends. Excellence in piloting a ship is not the same as excellence in medical treatment, as Plato's Socrates pointed out some centuries ago. Educational excellence cannot be achieved simply by imitating Berkeley or New Trier High School. For what purpose and in what way is excellence sought—to unfold the limited skills of the mentally retarded, to train a skilled medical diagnostician, to develop patience in teachers, to draw out the skills of a gifted musician, to educate persons to seek and find a newer world? Excellence is a many-splendored thing. Repetition of the word has no significance in itself despite attempts to use it like a magical incantation. For meaningful clarity, excellence must be related to purposes to be achieved and the methods of achieving them. If, taking its usual meaning of academic agility, all colleges attempt to become instant Harvards or creeping Carletons, then the competition for the "best" students and the richest donors to make such narrow excellence possible will be won only by the swift and the suave. There are other needs that higher education is meeting, other modes of excellence to be pursued, and many more areas where attention of high quality could be well given. Church-related colleges must draw from their broad heritage notions of excellence akin to Amos and Isaiah, to Jesus and St. Francis, to John Woolman and Jane Addams, as well as to Albert Einstein and Norbert Wiener.

Deliberate attention, for example, must be given in American education to the large number of students who fall in the middle range of abilities. By circumstance, more than by choice, church-related colleges have been serving this group. They ought to strive for genuine excellence in so doing. The importance of these persons for the overall quality of society has been vastly underestimated. To educate them for social sensitivity and involvement has potentialities only beginning to be realized. In a democratic society, social change depends not only on innovative leadership but equally on an informed electorate prepared to support such leadership. Colleges that have programs in urban affairs, in black studies, in ecology, and in social change, aimed at the students of moderate abilities, which engage students with actual situations and train them in the realities of party politics, are making an important contribution toward a better society.

There is also the group in American society who are now in their late thirties or in their forties who missed out on the opportunity for higher education resulting from the expansion of the 1950s. Persons in this group are often trapped in dead-end occupations—bus drivers, policemen, hard-hat jobs—and suffer great frustration as a result.[1] They are often the eager and bitter supporters of right-wing political figures. They endorse repressive police power and the suppression of dissent. Church-related colleges, because of their close community involvements, can launch programs of significant quality for this disadvantaged group.

By seeking varieties of excellence, church-related colleges can perform vital functions in society. Such activities will take on even greater importance if these colleges continue, without narrowly sectarian overtones, to draw on the resources of the Judeo-Christian faith in order to uncover societal needs and to move creatively in response. Technological innovations are more likely to occur in the heavily financed laboratories of the federal grant universities, but sensitivity to social justice and striving to make the world more fit for human habitation are areas in which church colleges are especially well equipped to join with concerned persons in other educational institutions as well as in society at large. Excellence as a sloganized cliché produces confusion. A college must discover how it wishes to excel in relation to which constituencies. Only when the crisis of identity has been resolved can the quest for excellence take on force and meaning.

2. Changing Purposes in Higher Education

To ask the question of purpose in higher education is not to anticipate easy agreement or even an eventual consensus around a single goal or function to which all colleges and universities ought to conform. Not even totalitarian societies have been able to coerce agreement among students and faculty. Clearly it would be impossible in such a heterogeneous and democratic society as the United States.

---

[1] See Adam Walinsky, "Four Political Illusions." *Humanity*, November, 1968.

Even more it would be inimical to the creativity that is essential to any education beyond rote learning.

Probably there is no single purpose nor one function that can do justice to the diverse character of higher learning as it has developed in Western society. Much of the rich creativity of the scholarly community has been illustrated in and is a product of its wide-ranging variety. And too, some of the most fascinating episodes of yesteryear and today transpired around the conflicts over purpose and function.

These conflicts are part of "the great goals battle," the continual struggle over what purposes will be served and what means will be utilized to achieve these ends. Much of the perpetual skirmishing over curriculum change, a favorite indoor sport of faculty, is part of the larger battle over the purposes of education and, along with it, who will control the process leading to the intended goals.

As the fecundity of higher education has led to expanded functions and greater involvement with many sectors of society, an increasing number of constituencies, some on campus but more off campus, have felt a stake in the educational process and in one way or another have joined in the battle over goals. The tempo of the struggle has risen steadily since World War II and reached a noisy crescendo in the protest movements and countermovements of the sixties. In that crowded, tragic decade the conflict did not revolve exclusively around a particular college or university and its purposes. Instead, partly because of the national character of the issues at stake and partly because of the expanded function and nearly instantaneous nature of the communications media, the battle raged across the land with similar constituencies—students, administrators, public officials, police—in various sectors of the country allied on a nationwide basis. As the nation as a whole participated in the mourning and the funeral ritual for President Kennedy, so constituencies with interests in higher education confronted one another nationally in the protests against the war in Southeast Asia.

The struggle over purpose and function is not new. Certainly the kinds of educational modification now in process are not without precedent. According to Veysey,[2] American higher education has

---

[2] Laurence R. Veysey, *The Emergence of the American University*. Chicago: University of Chicago Press, 1965.

gone through at least three major changes, utilizing four basic paradigms to understand its purpose and function. The colonial colleges and those before the Civil War saw themselves as cultivators of discipline and piety. Formulated earlier by Franklin and Jefferson, the notion of service and utility came to prominence after the Morrill Act of 1862. In the last quarter of the nineteenth century, the conception of higher education as basically for research entered the American scene from the German universities. Service and research were combined and entered upon a marriage of convenience and of love that shaped in measure the great expansion of higher education, financed first by the new industrial wealth and then increasingly by state and federal money. The older paradigm governed by ideals of discipline and piety was displaced but was formulated anew and repristinated in the educational paradigm of liberal culture. Now another paradigm is emerging, that of action or social change as central to the purpose and functioning of college and university education.

While change is not new to higher learning, education related intentionally to action on social issues and preparing persons to participate and lead in societal change is new. Educational styles and curricula tend still to be shaped by older paradigms, but another pattern of education is struggling to be born in colleges and universities not only in this country but also in other parts of the world. Sharp criticism is being leveled at existing education, based as it is on purposes from the past. Much talk is going around about "the crisis in education." Many creative suggestions and projections in regard to future forms of education are being made.

We are still, however, far from clear on certain crucial issues. Among these are: (1) what is the basic meaning of this emergent pattern; (2) what are appropriate programs for education directed toward social change; (3) what are the educational methods and experiences appropriate for such education; (4) what relationships ought to be sought between action education and older styles; and (5) what patterns of organization, governance, and funding are compatible with such innovation? No attempt will be made here to explore all these issues in detail. We shall try only to say enough to emphasize the importance of action education for church-related colleges as they reach for new and viable identities.

3. Education for Social Change

One of the most important ways for the church-related college to come to a new sense of identity and purpose is to extend the long tradition of Christian social concern into self-conscious involvement with social policy in the sectors of society to which college constituencies relate and to develop educational patterns to support that involvement, that is, education for social change. This means more than producing students with enlightened social attitudes and the ability to perform expert social analysis. Beyond and including attitudes and analysis, education for social change requires the interaction of students and faculty with situations and leaders in society, involves the combining of commitment, expertise, and leadership, and aims at reshaping the policies that inform societal processes. Harold Howe, former U.S. Commissioner of Education, in 1967, gave this stirring call to involvement:

> In this century and in this decade, our educational institutions cannot remain isolated from their communities; good fences do not make good neighbors, either on our urban or our rural campuses. The American university cannot be a withdrawn, uninvolved intellectual enclave while there is violence in our streets and still expect the populace to give it both support and freedom. . . .
> Our universities must become part of the action. They must turn all their resources and facilities to the problems of the survival of the communities of mankind—whether the community embraces a particular localized area or a state or whether it encompasses the nation as a whole or is worldwide.[3]

Colleges are already involved with social policy to a much greater degree than is usually known. Teachers, professionals, businessmen, and others, many of whom will be leaders in their vocations, are trained in colleges and are in part acquiring there the vision and skills in varying measure that they will use once they graduate. To become more self-conscious about social policy will enable a college to do better what it is already doing. Social policy does not refer only to the actions of the national government and its agencies but also to the policies of all institutions in society on local, regional, and national levels insofar as they shape the public arena in which all of us live.

---

[3] Quoted in "Howe Appeals for University Action to Help Save Cities," *The Chronicle of Higher Education*, August 23, 1967, p. 3.

Nor do concern for social policy and education for social change necessarily imply radical aims or methods. While it is always appropriate to remain aware of the importance of economic and political interests, it is also crucial that liberal, moderate reformist, or even conservative constituencies be served by such education. For example, one college, faced with the possibility of having to move to another city because of an economic depression in the area where it was located, decided instead to involve itself with social policy; it worked closely with local industry and civic leaders to develop ideas and resources for economic recovery. The effort was successful and the college grew along with the rejuvenated community, receiving from its involved and grateful leaders more acceptance and support than ever before.

Not only is awareness of involvement with social policy important in developing the identity of a college, so also is self-conscious selection of the sectors and levels of this involvement. On the one hand, there is a wide range of possibilities in society. Some of these correspond obviously to functions already existing in the college, e.g., politics and economics, business administration, computer science, education. Other sectors in society may suggest new programs the college ought to consider opening, e.g., urban affairs, ethnic studies, international experiences. No college can do everything, and selectivity must be exercised with such criteria operative as usefulness in relation to particular constituencies or accessible constituencies and the availability of resources. Careful research must be maintained on governmental programs, industrial interests, foundation grants, church agencies, etc., not in order to dash in uncritically for any funds available but to match potential resources with the needs and interests of college constituencies. The range of alternatives within which selectivity can be exercised should be kept as wide as possible. Nor are resources to be conceived only in financial terms. Locations for internships, exposure to certain situations, or assisting in projects of educational value may extend the opportunities available to students and others in ways more valuable than cash grants.

Levels of social policy involvement are also a matter for choice. Political possibilities range from local levels of voter registration and precinct organization to national conventions, Congress, the White House, the Supreme Court, and the United Nations. In education, policy concerns exist in local schools, on the district level, in PTA groups, in matters confronting school boards and teachers' groups, and in legislatures and the federal government. The same is true in every other sector. Not all levels of involvement with policy are open to every college or are appropriate to its educational purposes. On the other hand, the same selection process must take place concerning the sector and level of the college to be related to possibilities in society. It is neither necessary nor appropriate that the college as a whole or central sectors such as trustees or president be related to every activity. Just as a department of education might supervise a teacher-training program and a German society might sponsor a trip to Europe, so also it may be well to have it clearly established that the radical Student Union and not the dean sponsors involvement in social policy by means of demonstrations at the Pentagon, that the Black Studies Program and not the trustees sponsors the campus appearance of a Black Panther leader. Not all involvements which have important educational significance for the participants need be functions of the college as a whole.

Higher education is especially well equipped for responsible social policy involvement through its capacity for policy research. Social policy refers to the ordering and changing of priorities and resources in sectors of society shaping the public sphere by means of which patterns of actions are formed and projected in government, business, mass communication, churches, etc.; policy research denotes the cross-disciplinary enterprise that illumines policy alternatives, the ethical significance of different actions, and combines reflection over ends sought with the means of achieving them.[4] Concern for social policy, therefore, not only relates education to sectors of societal dynamism and decision but also encourages the hitherto isolated departments and programs of the college to draw on each other—an urban affairs program relating to ethnic studies, business administration, political science, and religious studies as these relate to the complexities of urban society; or teacher-training programs making use of sociology, economics, and public administration in dealing with educational policy. As Martin Tarcher rightly insists, knowledge is relational and cannot be fitted into academic

---

[4] See Kenneth Underwood, *The Church, the University and Social Policy.* Middletown: Wesleyan University Press, 1969.

compartments. "So long as we ignore the comprehensiveness of all things," he writes, "so long as we continue to divide our institutions into clearly defined and delimited departments and cram each department with sharply defined and delimited specialties, we shall continue to graduate men and women alienated from the realities of their time." [5]

While the humanization of society is not the exclusive concern of Christians, education for change and liberation seems an especially appropriate way for church-related colleges to combine their religious heritage with societal involvement. Not all church-related colleges are exercising their resources fully in areas of social policy and change. Quite clearly, it would be a loss to the colleges, to the churches, and to society, if the social concerns of the Hebrew-Christian tradition were not used to inform educational programs and to guide these colleges in using their strategic locations in communities throughout the nation to educate students and societal leaders for responsible roles in humanizing the environment.

4. Education for Responsibility

In *Personal Knowledge,* a work that opens a new era in human thought, Michael Polanyi demonstrates how passion and interest are necessary components in the process of knowing and learning. Since the Copernican revolution, Polanyi suggests, Western man has pursued "a mistaken ideal of objectivity." [6] Reflecting on this insight, we can see that the objectivist fallacy has permeated not only much of the academic research of the past two centuries but also the conception of education that has shaped campus processes. The importance of involvement and action for learning has been made use of primarily on the elementary and secondary levels. Here, however, it appears that the insight has tended to serve training for trivia rather than training for the important tasks of man in society. The Montessori schools are an important exception in regard to younger children. Education with the involvement that produces personal depth must be utilized by colleges and universities in the

---

[5] Martin Tarcher, "Leadership: Organization and Structure." Quoted in H. Lynn Jondahl, *Unrest on the Campus: A Christian Perspective.* New York: Friendship Press, 1970, p. 93.

[6] Michael Polanyi, *Personal Knowledge.* Chicago: University of Chicago Press, 1958, p. 7.

central areas of the liberal arts curriculum, as well as what we usually call vocational training. Indeed, it is my point here that it is only through such education that students will acquire the responsibility implied in taking up a calling, a vocation. In this more important sense of providing a context in which the student will find himself being called into responsibility, the church-related college must engage in vocational education through the whole range of its curriculum.

Certain types of learning obviously require action as part of the educational process. No one would attempt seriously to teach a student to play the piano by having him engage exclusively in the study of books about piano playing. But this is only one side of the issue. The other side has been a more difficult lesson for educators. It is that the learning of the apparently more abstract subjects such as philosophy, history, and sociology, and especially religion and literature, with personal depth requires involvement and action. Papers and examinations have been pale and ineffectual substitutes in these areas of study for projects that require one to make use of the subject matter and thereby compel appropriation of it into the student's total way of thinking and living. Recently, partly because activist students have applied pressure and partly because many educators have become eager to deepen the learning process, interesting innovations in educational methods have been taking place that devise means for confronting the student with real rather than paper problems and demand of him creativity in bringing varied academic resources to bear on human problems and appropriate resources to them. These new procedures may involve a simulated context for dealing with real problems close at hand; they may involve task forces in an urban ghetto or among the urban disadvantaged; they may involve supervised internships in social service agencies or government offices; they may require full-time work as apprentices in industrial or managerial situations. Whatever the source of the problem, whether it is dealt with on campus or in some distant location, the emphasis is on learning through grappling with real needs and problems.

The advantages of such a process of involved action are clearly the more vivid insight into a situation and a greater appropriation of the meaning used in shaping solutions. But also there is the acquiring of the personal commitments we call vocation. Quite often this will undoubtedly mean vocation in the weak sense as a way to earn a living. Under conditions of involved education, the possibility is greater that vocation as a way of committing the total self will emerge. The student tries out varied roles, comes into contact with persons having deep commitments, and enters into limited contracts that enable him to practice responsibility in a context of tasks and relationships. Peer relations in such a setting demand commitments to fellow students more congruent with life in society than do the settings of residence hall and extracurricular activities. The student may find meaningful life models other than those of professor or sports hero. In these ways education relating classroom and community places the student in environments of learning that open him to vocation on the deepest levels.

It is not hard to understand why colleges have given attention to education stressing the acquiring of information rather than developing abilities to lead and act innovatively in areas of social policy.[7] The former is far easier than the latter. But able, dedicated persons do lead and act in government, business, labor, and in social movements of all kinds. They learn in the process of taking on responsibility and having to make decisions. Educational institutions may learn from what is often called the "school of hard knocks" and incorporate parts of that well-known curriculum into their own programs. I have spoken already of education and campus governance. Now I shall extend that discussion by calling for comparable involvement in societal processes outside the campus.

Education seeking to develop in learners enhanced ability to combine commitment, expertise, and leadership in relation to social policy must have several components. At the core of such education is *participation and involvement* by learners in the context of real situations. There must be *interaction* with persons and groups related to the sectors of social policy about which learning is sought. *Mutual education* will be expected and encouraged among participants rather than the transmission of information exclusively to students. And finally *learning to attempt the new*, a seeking for the unknown, will be encouraged rather than learning only to repeat

---

[7] See R. Nevitt Sanford, *Where Colleges Fail.* San Francisco: Jossey-Bass, 1967.

responses and solutions already in use. Let us examine these elements more closely.

(1) *Participation and involvement.* The curriculum of action-oriented education will place students in contexts where social problems exist and policies relating to them are being formulated. They will experience the problems alongside persons who are actually wrestling with them and take on specific responsibilities for shaping and carrying out actions. In addition, they will be given help by faculty members and leaders in this societal sector in understanding the background, the present dimensions, and the perceived alternatives relevant to this societal sector, the problems being given attention, and the policies being applied. From those whose daily work already involves them will derive a sense of the commitment and urgency as well as knowledge of present realities. From faculty will come perspective and the resources of research. From student energy and freshness will emerge the potentiality of innovation curbed by real possibility. And from the experience of responsible participation will come the pressure to integrate knowledge and creativity into action. Issues of purpose and value will emerge in the process of allocating priorities in policy and action rather than in the abstractions of a class in ethics. Classes will not be eliminated but will occur in close relationship to problems with which students are involved and will take on freshness as faculty, students, and persons from the arena of participation wrestle together over goals set and actions being taken that are affecting human living.

(2) *Interaction.* Educational programs of this type will understand learning as taking place in a community of shared relations and responsibility rather than between a learner and certain facts. A context will be developed that places students in interaction with societal leaders and clients in sectors selected for attention, with academic experts in the faculty present and with other scholars through their writings, and with the great figures of the present and past who have thrown light on present issues. Such a context of interaction around present policies and actions intensifies involvement and provides greater motivation and processes of accountability than the artificial environment of isolated performance for grades in the traditional classroom.

The interaction between college and constituencies within such a curriculum would also increase the sense of relation between campus and community, develop more useful educational programs without eliminating academic resources and standards, and contribute to a greater awareness of institutional location and identity. The increased interaction might also widen the range of support for the college. Certainly leaders in business, government, ethnic groups, and education would appreciate the process and the problems of contemporary education as more contact with students and faculty took place. To the extent that these programs contributed to the formation of better social policy, entire communities and regions would benefit.

(3) *Mutual education.* In the model of education suggested here, learning will not be on the part of students alone, unless all participants in a program come to be regarded as students, a perception in large measure correct. Instead, the process will increasingly become a transaction in which students, faculty, and those involved from a particular sector of society learn from one another. Faculty nearly always are aware of mutual learning in ordinary classroom-type courses, and this transactional character is heightened in seminars and supervised practice. As education moves toward the action model, mutual education will increase. Faculty will find insight into immediate issues and alternatives extended by listening to persons involved in societal operations. These in turn will have their vision expanded and their acquaintance with research in their fields updated. Both will benefit from the fresh understanding of old problems and the new energies that students bring to such enterprises. Students will not only learn in the expected ways but will acquire skills of judgment passed on unconsciously as experts in a field act rather than talk about their action.

(4) *Learning to attempt the new.* Hidden within the interaction and mutual education inherent in this process lies a further possibility for which education always seeks but which usually hovers beyond reach of stereotyped classroom methods. That is the development of innovative capacities, the willingness to strike out beyond the practices of the present, the challenge to seek the unknown. This will come about not by magic but because this process places the three elements of scholarly resources, operational skills, and energetic freshness in juxtaposition rather than keeping them in-

sulated from one another. Apart from one another, each tends to grow stale and cynical. Scholarly research drifts off into academic warehouses where inert knowledge is stored. Operational skills become routinized into standard procedures, adequate for maintaining the organization over the short run but not for creative response to new problems. Then the energetic freshness of youth turns into carping cynicism or futile protest. Within a context of interaction, each may energize the other and produce a breakthrough to new levels of insight for all.

Such a pattern of education does not require that a college abandon the activities shaped by the paradigms of the transmission and advancement of learning. Rather it means building new programs that supplement and inevitably modify these older styles. Urban semesters, internships in business and government, independent projects in arenas of social dynamism already point toward the new curriculum. These have usually grown up without self-conscious relation to social policy and without developing carefully the interaction among students, faculty, and policy personnel envisaged in what we have said above. Movement outside the classroom walls is not enough. Only careful development of programs that place the student at the intersection of academic resource and participating action can elicit the learning that will combine commitment, expertise, and leadership. This education often takes place by accident. Colleges should try to help it happen by self-conscious design.

Interestingly enough, one area where such education has occurred is in the student protest movements of the past decade. Refused the right to infuse their innovative energies into social and educational reform through regular channels, young people organized movements compelling attention to their views. With much wasted motion and often with tragic interludes, the protest movements of the 1960s had important impact on higher education, on society, and especially on those who participated. It was learning of an intense and lasting nature for those involved.

The protests served an important purpose. They helped break frozen patterns of oppression in society and frozen patterns of educational process in colleges and universities. As history demonstrates repeatedly, protest can lift suppressed views into the public arena and thus help society respond to the pressures of the future. From the experiences of the protest decade, educators may find it possible to shape programs more responsive to the insights of students and the needs of the community.

Education modeled on these suggestions will not only contribute to forging a new identity for the church-related college but will also relate education to social change and the emerging problems of humanizing our world.

Chapter X

THE WAY AHEAD: TOWARD
IDENTITY AND RESPONSIBILITY

THOUGH THE FUTURE will not be smooth for church-related colleges, it is possible for most of them to find responsible roles and adequate resources. This means moving resolutely out of the sectarian past and conscious, planned involvement in the public present. It means also relating to change and social need through innovative educational programs and in the patterns of college governance. These are ways toward shaping a new identity and developing a deeper sense of responsibility. The way ahead, however, does not require a rejection of the past. Rather, it means building upon the heritage of relations and loyalties a responsiveness to the welfare of present and future constituencies. In particular, attention must be given to three areas: (1) a rethinking of the significance of the liberal arts; (2) cultivating mutually helpful relationships with the churches; and (3) developing centers for policy research and action on a cooperative basis.

1. Liberal Arts and Humanization

Higher education involves not one function but many: to transmit the cultural heritage, to do research and advance the frontiers of knowledge, to serve community needs—all these have been and continue to be valid. Now the function of action and advocacy is being added. This task requires becoming a change agent in society, self-consciously taking action for causes and groups aimed at enhancing the common good. Humanizing the world has always been at least an implicit purpose and indirect function of higher education. To shed restrictive remnants of sectarianism and don greater responsibility to the present means to take part intentionally in these purposes, letting the constituencies of the college aid in shaping its participation in education for social change and thereby reaching a significant sense of identity.

The church-related college as it seeks to resolve its crisis of identity must resist the temptation, powerful in some quarters today, to become a bastion of the liberal arts understood in a traditional sense. The stubborn hold of an older liberal arts tradition is one way an institution may have of guarding its alignments with upper economic groups related to Protestant churches and continuing, therefore, in revised form, its sectarian identity. The cost of operating such a college goes far to assure such alliances, and the conviction that traditional subjects are the best education for the churched and the genteel, concludes the compact. For the sake of its own integrity as well as the service it may perform, the church-related college must examine itself carefully at this point. On the one hand, it must offer academic curricula and financial opportunity that will support the vigorous recruitment of a wider socioeconomic spectrum of students. And on the other hand, it must develop innovative programs that will train its students from middle and upper economic levels for understanding and contending with the urgent problems of society.

Some may hold that these are not the functions of a liberal arts college, but such a conviction is based on a static notion of the liberal arts. Rather than regarding an authentically liberal education as enshrined in the old liberal arts college of the past with all change being viewed as a betrayal of that educational heritage, the liberal arts may be more properly regarded as education that liberates the human mind and prepares persons for coping with the problems of their world. The studies of history, of the Bible, and of Plato's *Dialogues* are irrelevant to the present only if they are studied as objects set in a distant time and place. Liberal education today should start with the problems of civil rights, urban problems, the ecological crisis, issues of international policy, and bring the wise resources of our heritage to bear upon these pressing issues.

A liberating education today must also widen its horizons to include international resources. With opportunities afforded by better transportation and communication, there is no reason to study other cultures only in textbooks. Travel seminars and time spent as students in Europe, Africa, and Asia will go further to bring about deep interaction with other cultures than will discussions about them on an isolated campus in the United States. The study of languages as the doorway into other cultures will always be inadequate so long as it is limited to three class periods per week focused on grammar. But this study will become jet-propelled when the student is placed on a street in Mainz or in a classroom in Moscow and required to immerse himself in a new linguistic and cultural context.

In a similar way, the experiences of blacks in an urban ghetto will become vivid for students when they have opportunities to work and live in a slum situation. The students' experiences will be enriched to the extent that studies of the black cultural heritage are offered in the college. We must cease being wedded to the myth of the well-rounded Renaissance man with training fitted for the rural gentleman now removed to the suburbs. Education so focused is not only out of date but would be unliberating and irrelevant for the students crowding into our colleges today.

Liberal arts education means the humanization of the student, making him aware of his world, developing his sympathies for problems and the plights of human beings today. Such education does not have a particular subject matter but instead will bring the resources of our heritage and the new learning of our world to bear on fitting students to be competent human beings in the societies of which they will be a part. The particular problems and subjects dealt with and the ways of teaching them must change with the new horizons and differing opportunities of every age. The possibilities for the liberal arts today are exciting when one sees such education as related to human need, rapid change, and social policy.

Just as liberal arts education means humanization, so also humanization means discovering who one is, finding one's identity.[1] Because our social matrix shapes us in the identities of the past, it is the special task of higher education to aid in shaping identities for the present and the future. To discover who we are today requires that we understand the revolutions and technology of the present,

---

[1] Cf. Arthur W. Chickering, *Education and Identity*. San Francisco: Jossey-Bass, 1969.

that we respond to the rising expectations among the disadvantaged around the world, and that we educate for change and the future.

But we have stated the problem as though the task of the college is aiding each student to find *his* identity. We mean to suggest further that in responding to the needs of the present and in developing educational patterns aligned with these needs, the college will discover a new identity for itself. Pursuit of a curriculum based on liberal arts conceived as liberation and humanization can contribute to greater self-understanding not only for students but for the whole college community.

2. College and Church

What is the new relation of church and college to be as the college seeks for a new identity? Often the issue is seen to be whether or not to sever all church ties. This is not the productive question, but rather what kind of relations are appropriate—which ties to cut, which ones to alter or develop, what new relations to form? To continue old sectarian controls would be death. But to sever all ties would be harmful to churches and colleges and to society at large.

One clarification is in order at this point, one which applies to everything said about the contribution of church-related colleges to society. Many hold, either by intention or through inadvertence, that the purpose of religion is to serve and enhance the society of which it is a part. In particular a criterion often applied to Christianity in the United States is its usefulness to American society. Some would even deny to the churches the right to be critical of national policies and goals. Let me dissociate myself from these and similar views. While it is true that religion does serve to bind personal, social, and cultural action systems into a whole, it also provides both the legitimation of and critical perspective upon the value structure and goals of these systems. The Judeo-Christian heritage and the institutions in American society that purport to embody that heritage have contributed much to that society and will continue to do so, but they do not exist to serve that society. The purposes they serve are rooted in a wider reality than is encompassed in any one society, and the faith which empowers that heritage is constantly transcending the values of every particular social group. Those who would judge churches by their contribution to the national values and purposes betray that heritage and announce their real religion to be nationalism. We may push the point even further and say that the most important contribution the churches make to American society is through their critique of cultural norms. Such a critique impels a society toward the continuing change and permanent revolution essential to its development. Though churches have often tended to endorse the status quo, groups inspired by Judeo-Christian faith have been continuing as crucial sources of protest, criticism, and change in the United States.

College and church today have opportunities as never before to develop productive interaction. On the one hand, churches may provide channels to extend the contact of colleges into all sectors of society and committed energies as resource for all levels of college activity. On the other hand, colleges can supply educated persons for church participation and the continuing resources of academic learning and insight for all aspects of church life.

When colleges develop innovative educational programs, a major resource can be the persons, institutions, and situations to which church-relatedness provides access. Though it would be a mistake to use only contacts through churches, it would be a major error not to utilize these channels.

Student groups often gain access to interesting sectors of urban life through parishes and seminaries—for example, through Glide Memorial Church and Pacific School of Religion in the San Francisco-Berkeley area or through Judson Memorial Church and Union Theological Seminary in New York. But the possibilities are much wider. Internships in government, business, and the arts can be located if church channels are seen in terms of laity no less than clergy. Resources for educational planning might be extended from the imaginative personnel in public relations, politics, and the arts. College reorganization and funding can be aided by corporation executives and management consultants. The list could be continued, limited only by time and imagination. The major point is that channels into society, including the churches, must be seen and used as more than reservoirs of money. These channels can provide endless enrichment for educational programs. Involvement of such persons and institutions can also open sources of funding unavailable before.

The church, viewed as channel of access, can become a vital part of the college relating itself to society. But the benefit would be mutual, not one-way.

In this era of increasing complexity and rapidly developing technology, churches and churchmen need more than devotion and commitment to take action on behalf of change that will make the world more human. The church-related college is increasingly becoming a resource for churches as they seek to engage society on its creative edge of change. Father John Walsh has stated it this way:

> To think of the Catholic university as an instrument of the Church for the carrying out of its *teaching* mission leads, I think, both to serious misunderstanding of the Church's teaching mission in itself and to profound distortions of the nature of a university. . . . It appears to me that the generic relationship between the Church and the Catholic university is one of the manifestations—perhaps the highest formal, explicit, and systematic manifestation—of the Church *learning.*[2]

Churches must have close ties with higher education if the resources of new knowledge and skills are to shape the ministries the contemporary world requires. No longer is it possible to rely on catechetical classes and Sunday schools—and was probably never either wise or possible—for the preparation of ministers, lay and clerical, for the diverse needs of society. Colleges and universities—church-sponsored, private, and public—are required for the enormous and varied challenges of ministry in our complex and changing world. Two functions, at least, are essential: first, the education of youth who have some grasp of contemporary society and culture and who therefore have the potential for leadership in ministry; and second, to provide the technical knowledge and expert skills required for ministry. This is no time for cutting ties between churches and colleges but rather for developing closer relationships of mutual criticism and cooperation.

Such a view of mutual relationship has implications for the relation of church agencies to church-sponsored colleges. The older attempts at sectarian control, which in most cases are no longer possible, must be abandoned. Colleges will be useful to churches only

---

[2] John E. Walsh, C.S.C., "The University and the Church," in Edward Manier and John W. Houck (eds.), *Academic Freedom and the Catholic University.* Notre Dame, Indiana: Fides Publishers, 1967, pp. 108, 109.

as they participate in the marketplace of academic freedom and performance. Nor should funds from church agencies be allocated without priorities to any college bearing the denominational name. Instead, church agencies ought to use their limited financial resources: 1) as grants for specific projects, which colleges may seek by application; 2) to encourage joint planning and action with other colleges to strengthen the educational process; 3) to provide for development of programs that prepare youth to become sensitive and experienced agents of change whether their ministries will be in ecclesiastical or public positions; and 4) to encourage the development of social policy research and education that will provide resources for churches and public groups in understanding the human needs today and acting to improve the human lot.

The task of the churches in higher education has not been completed. But more than losses in the present are at stake in maintaining church-college ties. Many contributions of churches and church-related colleges to higher education are yet to be made. If colleges and churches sever their ties, what will be lost is not the past nor the present but the future.

3. Policy Research and Action[3]

All that has been suggested in the previous section and much that has been said earlier depend upon developing better resources for educational planning, funding, and involvement with social change. This can be done through policy research and through action based upon such research. To the extent that college and church take seriously their responsibilities to one another and to society, they must undertake policy research and development bearing on their internal operations and on social policy. At no point is there greater potential for cooperation among colleges and between colleges and various sectors of church life.

Leadership in church and in church-related college tends still to rely far too much upon intuition and charisma. Neither ought to be underestimated, but leadership today requires the uniting of commitment, knowledge, and the power of decision, for action in

---

[3] See Kenneth Underwood, *The Church, the University and Social Policy,* for further information on the meaning and potentiality of centers of policy research and action.

society. It is for this reason that church agencies and church-related colleges must place highest priority on the joint development of centers for policy research and action. This enterprise should be undertaken on an ecumenical basis with the participation of major church agencies, charitable foundations, and colleges organized into regional groupings. Joint funding efforts may form the nucleus of these consortia, but the central purpose of such a center is policy planning.

Social involvement on the part of college or church must include the development of policy alternatives, expertise for the analysis of complex courses of action and probable results, and a comprehensive information system. These are needed to inform action, lest good intentions and firm commitment be wasted. Centers for policy research and action can provide these components, and colleges, working with leaders in church and society, have the resources to develop such centers.

Colleges need policy research in many ways, but especially to provide information on government programs and potential funding sources, and on educational opportunities and innovation. So much of such data applies to all colleges that it is senseless to have duplication and fumbling because of ineffectual individual efforts. While analysis of problems and development of policy alternatives can be done better on a cooperative basis, the execution of policies must be done through specific organizations. The need for informed leadership remains. Because the output from a center for policy research and action would be as useful to church agencies and executives as to colleges, there is probably no single area where joint efforts and cooperative funding would achieve greater mutual advantage.

4. An Open Future

The crucial task of the church-related college today is resolving the identity crisis so as to meet the demands of the public present and at the same time affirm its Christian heritage. To the extent that it holds on to its sectarian past it will find itself on the periphery of contemporary society and limited to a declining proportion of the population from which to recruit students and faculty. If it breaks its ties completely with its heritage and becomes another secularized institution, then it can no longer be regarded meaning-

163

fully as church-related. I have been attempting to sketch a line of action between these alternatives.

My analysis has rejected as fallacious a solution based on an attempt to be unique. Besides pointing out the impossibility of the operational uniqueness, I have tried to state a Christian theological basis for abandoning the pursuit of uniqueness and affirming the solidarity of the college with the communities to which it is related. In various ways the conception of the college building itself through interrelations with the community around has been elaborated as the key to a new identity for the church-related college and a new awareness of responsibility.

Education in this perspective brings the resources of the past and the innovative insight of contemporary experimentation and research to bear on human needs and social tasks. The ivory tower has always been a scholarly illusion. Now the college is called to celebrate its existence within society and to find its life through participation. On the one hand, to function in this way requires shaping education in close interrelation with the communities around, locally and regionally, nationally and globally conceived. On the other hand, it does not mean conforming to the requests of society but rather preparing leaders to deal critically and innovatively with problems of the human community. Working closely with societal leaders and spokesmen for the disadvantaged will keep the college attuned to genuine needs and also gain the confidence and support of the community. Resources from society will be more easily available for education, and greater understanding of the necessity for freedom and even eccentricity within the academic community will be more easily communicated. If the examination of different and even unpopular ideas can be shown as essential to discovering innovative solutions to problems plaguing society, then academic freedom will be welcomed rather than merely tolerated or suppressed.

The entire college, as its life interpenetrates the community, becomes the arena of education. The classroom becomes open to articulate persons from the community. The learning process enters into and participates in the community. The college does not operate as an enclave but becomes a resource for industry and ghetto, public school and social service agency; it becomes a center for planning in various areas of society as it works with community groups and prepares students to take their places in this society.

To carry out these possibilities, I have made these suggestions:

1. The church-related college must study the perceived and real needs of communities it touches, delineate precisely those it has resources with which to grapple, and take steps in concert with appropriate community leaders toward assuming educational responsibility in relation to them. In choosing the tasks to which the college will devote itself, the criterion of furthering the welfare and interests of the human community should be central. But involvement with the genuine and limited purposes of real constituencies is essential if the college is to find its public and Christian functions.

2. Rather than deploring the disadvantages today of a denominational background, the church-related college should seek cooperation with other denominational colleges in ways that will enhance the resources of the individual colleges and develop an ecumenical coalition within higher education that can add significant dimensions to the educational process in American society. This cooperation may be varied—recruitment and admissions procedures, combined library resources, shared faculty, joint purchasing and bookkeeping, common urban and international programs. Such cooperation will undoubtedly attract financial support, federal and other. The range of possibility is wide, and the potentiality for improved education with innovative ecumenical dimensions vast.

3. By moving toward a self-conscious diversity within its campus structures, by taking up varied social tasks and finding curricular forms for coping with them, and by making full use of ecumenical relationships, the church-related college may contribute substantially to the educational environment dominated by state institutions. Not only by maintaining a creative diversity but also by pioneering new modes of education can church-related colleges contribute. The heritage of Christian concern places these colleges in an especially advantageous position for shaping new ways to involve students productively with the needs of the human community. The motivation will be strengthened with the recognition that new forms of education will not only deal with community problems but will also provide ways for making college training an arena of meaning and vocation for students. New dimensions will be added to the educational process as the campus widens itself to include the points of crisis and the centers of agony within society.

4. A primary instrument for coming to grips with all the areas

of innovation mentioned is the conversion of the college into a community of authority in which the decisions about campus rules, curriculum, and administrative policy are included in the process of training for responsibility and action. No less than the entire college provides education for its members, and it is the shape of the total community to which attention must be given in order to improve the quality of preparation offered and the theological dimensions of the process.

5. And finally, cooperation between college and church ought to be continued and extended, no longer with attempts from one side or the other to control, but as partners in mutually helpful ways. Of highest priority in such cooperation is the development of joint centers of policy research and action to inform leadership and programs in both college and church.

In these ways, the future is open for church-related colleges. They are called to affirm rather than resist their public present and to do so through a new vision of what their Christian heritage demands. The ministry of Jesus Christ will not be fulfilled by adding religious activities at the edges of campus life and student involvement but by developing Christian ministry from the center of the college and striving to have that ministry permeate the entire educational process. Discovering purposes and functions that render education responsive to the needs of the human community and carried on by involving the entire college in interaction with societal constituencies is the path toward a new identity for the church-related college and the development of the responsible campus.

INDEX OF NAMES

167